THE OVERSEERS

The Overseers

Public Accounts Committees and Public Spending

DAVID G. MCGEE, QC

Commonwealth Parliamentary Association
in Association with
Pluto Press
London • Sterling, Virginia

First published 2002 by Pluto Press
345 Archway Road, London N6 5AA
and 22883 Quicksilver Drive, Sterling, VA 20166-2012, USA

www.plutobooks.com

Copyright © 2002 Commonwealth Parliamentary Association

The right of David G. McGee to be identified as the author of this work has been asserted by him in accordance with the Copyright, Designs and Patents Act 1988

British Library Cataloguing in Publication Data

A catalogue record for this book is available from the British Library

Library of Congress Cataloging in Publication Data

A catalog record for this book has been requested.

ISBN 0 7453 1986 6 hardback

Designed and produced for Pluto Press by
Curran Publishing Services, Norwich

Printed and bound in Great Britain by
Antony Rowe Ltd, Chippenham, Wiltshire

Contents

Foreword	ix
List of members of the Study Group	xi
Introduction	1
Background	1
Study Group convened	2
Meetings of the Study Group	3
Objectives of the Study Group	4
Conclusions and recommendations	5
The Public Accounts Committee as part of democratic accountability	9
Democracy and accountability	9
What is accountability?	10
Public Accounts Committees and Auditors-General	11
Status of PACs and Auditors-General	12
The cost of accountability	13
The international dimension	15
Greater inter-dependency	15
Creditworthiness of nations	15
Changing nature of lending	16
Contact between PACs and international lenders	18
International corruption	18
Auditors-General	21
Appointment	22
Term of office	24

Renewability of term	24
Removal from office	25
Recruitment and training of staff	26
Training for Auditors-General	28
Auditor-General's relationships	28
Executive	28
Legislature	30
Public Accounts Committees	31
Working practices	32
The role of the Auditor-General	34
Standards	34
Internal audit	35
Performance evaluation	36
Environmental and gender impact auditing	39
Budget reporting	40
Central bank auditing	41
Choosing a work programme	41
Audit independence	41
Legislative influence	42
Risk assessment	43
Budget and resources	43
IT developments	45
Legal powers and immunities	45
Extent of the Auditor-General's remit	47
Privatisation	47
Government's shareholding interests	48
Corporatisation and service delivery	49
Commercial confidence	50
Reporting	51
Preparation of reports	51
Reporting to Parliament	52
Follow-up to reports	53
Audit performance	53
Public Accounts Committees	55
The role of the PAC	55

Other committees	56
Relationship with the Auditor-General	56
Aspects of a PAC's terms of reference	58
Status of the PAC	59
Membership of the PAC	61
Training	62
Chair of PAC	65
Manner of appointment	65
Government/opposition chairs	66
Role	66
Resources	68
Examination of policy	69
Unanimity	71
Working practices	71
Frequency of meetings	71
Meeting in public or in private	72
Subcommittees	73
Witnesses	74
Reporting	75
Findings	76
Recommendations in PAC reports	78
Follow-up to reports	78
Responses	78
Implementation	79
Debate	80
Problems for developing countries and smaller Parliaments	**83**
Resources	83
Attendance of members	85
Lack of legal protections	87
Lack of understanding of PAC's role	87
Information exchanges	**89**
Role of the CPA	89
Individual websites	90
News groups	91
Conferences and meetings	92

Compendium of PAC practice	93
Benchmarking	94

Appendices:

1 Results of questionnaire on Public Accounts Committees   95

2 Battling corruption: strengthening Parliament's oversight role. Forty-seventh Commonwealth Conference, plenary session summary, Canberra, Australia, September 2001   105

3 Strengthening Parliament's role in the battle against corruption. Forty-seventh Commonwealth Conference, workshop report, Canberra, Australia, September 2001   109

Foreword

The Commonwealth Parliamentary Association has a long-established practice of bringing together small gatherings of Parliamentarians to take an in-depth look at an aspect of democratic and parliamentary processes. These Study Groups, as they are called, give careful consideration to their subject of examination, and produce reports which the CPA disseminates across its membership and beyond as a contribution to assist in furthering the work of political practitioners and those interested in democratic institutions.

In 1999 a CPA Study Group reported on 'Parliamentary Committees: Enhancing Democratic Governance', which stressed the role of committees in parliamentary oversight and scrutiny. Recognising that Parliament's most important committee in the area of oversight and scrutiny is undoubtedly the Public Accounts Committee (PAC), a decision was taken by the CPA Executive Committee to commission a Study Group to consider how PACs function in the Parliaments of the Commonwealth, and, in the best CPA tradition, to share experience so as to assist all.

As an organisation of over 170 Parliaments and legislatures and more than 16,000 members in 51 of the 54 countries of the Commonwealth, the CPA is uniquely equipped to commission such a study. I am grateful to the group of senior members listed below, and the advisers and observers who participated with them, for their work which has resulted in this Report. Participation by Auditors-General or their representatives and by an official of the World Bank Institute, with which the CPA has successfully collaborated in the area of parliamentary oversight of the Executive, resulted in valuable contributions.

Meetings of the Study Group were held in the Legislative Building of the Legislative Assembly of Ontario at Queen's Park, Toronto, and I extend the thanks of the CPA to Hon. Gary Carr, MPP, Speaker of the Legislative Assembly of Ontario, and to the Clerk and Staff of the Assembly for their warm hospitality and assistance throughout.

The proceedings of the Study Group have been distilled by Mr David McGee, QC, Clerk of the House of Representatives of New Zealand, into this report, which I am confident will become a valuable document for all those interested in the manner in which the Parliaments of the Commonwealth hold their governments to account. I extend thanks to Mr McGee and to my colleagues Mr Raja Gomez and Mr Anthony Staddon, respectively CPA's Director and Assistant Director of Development and Planning, for their work in organizing a successful meeting.

The result of the work of the Study Group will be a further significant contribution by the CPA as we continue our efforts to enhance the performance of Parliaments and Parliamentarians and improve the public perception of parliamentary institutions.

Arthur R. Donahoe, QC
Secretary-General
Commonwealth Parliamentary Association
1993–2001

List of members of the Study Group

Hon. Bernard Chen, MP (Singapore)	South-East Asia
Hon. M. G. K. Mooka, MP (Botswana)	Africa
Mr Andrew Rowe, MP (UK)	British Isles and the Mediterranean
Hon. Ginson Saonu, MP (Papua New Guinea)	Pacific
Mr Audley Shaw, MP (Jamaica)	Caribbean, Americas and the Atlantic
Shri N D Tiwari, MP (India)	Asia
Senator the Hon. John Watson (Australia)	Australia
Mr John Williams, MP (Canada)	Canada

TECHNICAL ADVISERS

Mr Michael McLaughlin Deputy Auditor General, Canada)
Mr Erik Peters (Provincial Auditor, Ontario)
Mr Vinod Sahgal (The World Bank Institute)

OBSERVERS

Miss Jennifer Edwards, MP (Jamaica)
Mr Repe Rambe (Secretary, Public Accounts Committee, Papua New Guinea)
Dr Mohd. Tap Salleh (Commonwealth Secretariat)

Mrs Jocelyne Therrien (Office of the Auditor General of Canada)

RAPPORTEUR

Mr David McGee, QC (New Zealand)

CPA SECRETARIAT

Mr Arthur R. Donahoe, QC (Secretary-General)
Mr Raja G Gomez (Director, Development & Planning)
Mr Anthony Staddon (Assistant Director, Development & Planning)

Introduction

BACKGROUND

The Commonwealth Parliamentary Association's Strategic Plan for the period 1999–2002 includes, as a core objective, furthering the ability of members and branches to move towards the adoption of locally utilisable systems of good governance and to continue to contribute to the strengthening of Parliament. This objective embodies perhaps the most fundamental contribution that the CPA can make for its members and branches.

To this end the CPA is concentrating much of its work in the fields of oversight and scrutiny. Strong parliamentary oversight and scrutiny regimes are an essential part of combating corruption and promoting good governance generally; indeed they may be seen as an essential component of such aims. It is increasingly being recognised that effective parliamentary oversight depends upon an active committee system within the Parliament that allows members to penetrate below the surface of government administration and to make accountability real by promoting direct interaction between elected legislators and the civil service.

In 1997 and 1998 a CPA group carried out an in-depth study of parliamentary systems. Its proceedings and conclusions were published in 1999 (see *Parliamentary Committees: Enhancing Democratic Governance*). In 1998 the CPA held a seminar on governance structures and the democratic process, examining Commonwealth experience in oversight and scrutiny. The report that resulted from that seminar was widely acclaimed and used by several international organisations, including the World Bank.

This led directly to the World Bank and the CPA collaborating in early 2001 in building up a specialised volume of up-to-date writing analysing current experience in oversight and scrutiny and the effects on the relationship between Parliament and the Executive.

These moves at a 'macro' parliamentary committee level led to the view that they should be followed up by a study of how accountability can and does function at the level of a committee: in particular, in regard to the most well established, and for this purpose arguably the most important, parliamentary committee, the Public Accounts Committee. (The Public Accounts Committee is known by a number of variants of this title throughout the Commonwealth. It is convenient in this report to refer to it as the Public Accounts Committee or PAC.)

STUDY GROUP CONVENED

For this purpose, the CPA convened a Study Group consisting of the Secretary-General of the CPA and persons with experience as chairpersons and members of PACs from Australia, Botswana, Canada, India, Jamaica, Papua New Guinea, Singapore and the United Kingdom. The group met from 28–31 May in the Ontario Legislative Building, Toronto. The Ontario CPA Branch was responsible for hosting the group throughout its stay in Toronto and made the necessary arrangements most efficiently, receiving the group warmly. The CPA and the members of the Study Group are deeply appreciative of the efforts made on their behalf by the Ontario Branch.

As well as the members and former members of Commonwealth PACs who constituted the Study Group attending throughout the week, the group was also fortunate to enlist the participation of other persons as advisers and observers. These others played a full part in the group's deliberations and have made major contributions to the outcome of its work.

The CPA's collaboration with the World Bank in the area of Parliament's oversight relationship with the Executive has

INTRODUCTION

already been mentioned. A representative from the World Bank Institute was able to attend throughout the Study Group's meetings as a resource person. It is hoped that the Study Group's deliberations and report will assist the World Bank Institute in its endeavours to strengthen parliamentary oversight in a number of countries where it is sponsoring programmes.

The Commonwealth also has a longstanding interest in promoting good governance. The 1999 CHOGM communiqué recognised that corruption has become global in reach and that action at both a national and a local level is needed for it to be tackled comprehensively. For this reason the Study Group was pleased to have the assistance of an observer from the Commonwealth Secretariat throughout its meetings. It is hoped that the CPA's work will contribute to the initiatives being pursued through CHOGM and the Commonwealth Secretariat.

The Study Group was particularly grateful to enlist the support and assistance of the Office of the Auditor-General of Canada and of the Provincial Auditor of Ontario. The Deputy Auditor-General of Canada, the Provincial Auditor and a member of the Canadian Auditor-General's staff attended the week's meetings and presented papers. Given the fact that any study of the PAC inevitably encompasses a consideration of the role of the Auditor-General, this Auditor-General association with the work of the Study Group was invaluable.

Finally, the Study Group was supported by the Clerk of the House of Representatives, New Zealand, who acted as rapporteur and prepared drafts of this report, the secretary of the Papua New Guinea PAC, as an observer, and the Director and Assistant Director of the CPA's Development and Planning division.

MEETINGS OF THE STUDY GROUP

The Study Group meetings were opened on 28 May by the Secretary General of the CPA who also chaired the opening session. Thereafter sessions were chaired by members of the group in rotation. During the course of the week the Study Group met with the Chair of the Ontario legislature's PAC and benefited greatly from listening to his experiences in this area. It was also briefed by a representative from the Canadian Parliamentary Centre, Ottawa on the work of the centre, which is intimately involved in promoting the good governance issues with which the Study Group was concerned.

Prior to the Study Group's meetings the CPA Secretariat carried out a survey of all branches to obtain some hard data on the operation of PACs throughout the Commonwealth. The preliminary survey results contributed to the Study Group's discussions and are drawn on and referred to in this report. (The final survey results are set out in Appendix 1.) Each session of the group began with a presentation by a participant based on a paper that had already been distributed. The meeting was then opened for contributions from all participants, including advisers and observers.

The main topics covered during the eight sessions held by the group were:

- The state of the art in the Commonwealth
- The ecology of the PAC
- The Committee's purpose, scope and functions
- The structure of the PAC
- The Auditor-General and the PAC
- Special problems in small Parliaments
- Methods of committee operations
- Position of the PAC in the overall committee structure
- The PAC in the future.

OBJECTIVES OF THE STUDY GROUP

The purpose of the Study Group is to assess how PACs are working in practice and whether they are fulfilling expectations as important guarantors of good governance. The group has tried to distil the practices that it has discussed into checklists of considerations for Parliaments, always recognising that social, economic and political factors within each country mean that there is no one organisational form that a PAC will take. The group has also discussed and tried to define a modern rationale for PACs. This is necessitated by and is based on the international dimension that results from the much greater inter-dependability of nations today. In turn, this has resulted from the enormous increases in the speed of communication and in the volume of population movements that the world has experienced, and the lowering of trade and finance barriers, with consequent expansions in the international flows of goods and money. All this has brought in its wake greater challenges to good (and honest) government.

Consequently, this report takes the form of a discussion of a number of salient issues identified by the group during its deliberations: from higher-level considerations of accountability to more detailed matters concerned with PAC and Auditor-General roles and working practices. Special consideration is given to the particular problems that are experienced by smaller legislatures. Finally, some issues relating to international co-operation and information exchange are explored. The examples quoted in the text are taken from the Parliaments represented on the Study Group and the survey carried out by the CPA.

CONCLUSIONS AND RECOMMENDATIONS

The solutions to problems identified throughout the report are not necessarily applicable to all Parliaments. However, the report does try to identify possible courses of action to improve governance outcomes through more effective use of PACs and Auditors-General and through efforts at cross-national collaboration.

The Study Group's deliberations have convinced it that PACs are seriously committed to building their capacity and improving their own performance so that, as a consequence, better public sector accountability will result. The Study Group identified three main priorities for action, and these themes are discussed throughout this report:

- *Capacity building.* A constant theme is the need to improve institutional capability, that is, the ability of Parliaments, PACs and Auditors-General's offices to carry out their functions by being provided with sufficient resources and having adequate training and access to the expertise that they require.
- *Independence.* Particularly for Auditors-General it is essential that they be free from political or legal constraints that could inhibit them carrying out their duties diligently and impartially.
- *Information exchange.* PACs in particular need to have the means to exchange information and ideas so as to keep them up-to-date with important developments, changing standards and best-practices as they emerge.

The following are the main individual conclusions and recommendations of the Study Group:

- There should be greater direct contact between Parliaments, especially PACs, and international financial institutions (p. 18).
- The CPA include good government as a subject of the theme or sub-theme of its conferences (p. 19).
- The Auditor-General should be an Officer of Parliament independent of the Executive (pp. 22–3).
- The appointment process for an Auditor-General should involve consultation with a wide range of stakeholders (p. 23).
- An Auditor-General should only be removed from office on limited grounds that are specified in advance by law (pp. 25–6).
- Auditors-General should actively participate in international Auditors-General associations (p. 28).
- Auditors-General should actively introduce themselves and their services to all parliamentary committees, not just PACs (pp. 30–1).
- Auditors-General have a role in approving internal audit standards (p. 36).

INTRODUCTION

- Central banks should be subject to the Auditor-General's audit mandate in the same way as other public sector agencies (p. 41).
- The Auditor-General should not be prevented from inquiring into anything within the audit mandate (pp. 42–3).
- Auditors-General should take account of the views of PACs in framing their work programmes (pp. 42–3).
- Parliaments should be involved at the pre-Budget stage in determining the resources to be allocated to the Auditor-General (p. 44).
- Auditors-General and their staff must have appropriate legal protections conferred on them to enable them to carry out their duties (pp. 45–7).
- PACs should keep under review any proposals to change the Auditor-General's audit mandate (pp. 49–50).
- Any company receiving public funding to deliver public services should be subject to the Auditor-General's audit mandate in respect of those services (p. 50).
- Auditors-General should present their reports in an attractive form and devise active communications strategies (pp. 51–2).
- Auditors-General should take steps to measure their own performance (pp. 53–4).
- The main aim of the PAC's work should be guided by the work of the Auditor-General (p. 57).
- Parliaments should regard the PAC as their pre-eminent committee (p. 59).
- Senior opposition figures must be associated with the PAC's work (p. 61).
- There should always be sufficient experience and seniority among the membership of the PAC (p. 62).
- Specially structured training be provided to PAC members (pp. 64–5).
- It is crucial that the chairperson of the PAC has the qualities to ensure that the PAC works effectively (p. 66).
- PACs must be adequately resourced to carry out their functions (pp. 68–9).
- PACs, while not being bound to act unanimously, should strive for some consensus in their reports (p. 71).

- PACs should promote greater public awareness of their role (pp. 72–3).
- PACs should consider using subcommittees for specific inquiries (pp. 73–4).
- The Internet should be used to disseminate information on PACs (p. 75).
- Procedures for follow-up action on recommendations in PAC reports are critical (p. 78).
- Parliament should hold an annual debate on the work of the PAC (pp. 80–1).
- PACs in smaller and developing Parliaments need improved access to information technology (p. 84).
- A rational local method of allocating funding to PACs needs to be put in place to ensure that they have adequate resources (p. 84).
- Smaller Parliaments need to take innovative steps to expand the pool of personnel available to serve on the PAC (p. 85).
- Special attendance allowances, rather than a special salary, should be considered for PAC attendance (p. 86).
- Links between PAC websites should be developed (p. 91).
- The CPA should explore the potential for the use of a news group to encourage information exchange on PAC matters (pp. 91–2).
- The CPA should examine what options exist for conferences or associations of PACs (pp. 93–4).
- A compendium of Commonwealth PAC practice be established to be managed by a CPA branch or Parliament (p. 93).
- Research should be undertaken into establishing a basis for making international comparisons of PAC performance (p. 94).

The Public Accounts Committee as part of democratic accountability

DEMOCRACY AND ACCOUNTABILITY

The members and branches of the CPA are as diverse in their cultures as one would expect to find among peoples who represent a quarter of the world's population. What they are united in is an interest in promoting democracy through parliamentary systems, albeit systems that are very different in such things as their relationships with the Executive, their size and their methods of operation. How democracy is given expression within each of our societies varies enormously. But that we all share an interest in promoting it, and that it involves limitations on the exercise of governmental powers through the citizenry's ability to participate in government is, we take it, undoubted. The principle of parliamentary control of the public purse is well established among the branches of the CPA.

Democracy entails accountability for the exercise of power. Accountability has a huge number of facets. It is not just *post hoc* reporting, although this is part of it. Accountability also involves constructing appropriate systems that allow decisions to be taken in a context that promotes honesty and productivity. Nor is accountability reposed in any single institution or organisation. Our whole system of government – executive, legislative and judicial – is part of the accountability mechanisms existing within a state, as are other components of civil society such as the press and voluntary organisations.

Our Parliaments themselves have developed a number of means of subjecting the executive arm of government to accountability. Such procedures as questions, urgent debates, the estimates process, scrutiny of delegated legislation, private members' motions, and adjournment debates allow members to raise issues relating to the use or proposed use of governmental power, to call upon the government to explain actions it has taken, and to require it to defend and justify its policies or administrative decisions. The Public Accounts Committee is part of the parliamentary infrastructure that helps to ensure that governments account for their operating policies and actions, and their management and use of public resources.

WHAT IS ACCOUNTABILITY?

It is worth elaborating on the concept of accountability, to help one to draw conclusions about the adequacy or effectiveness of PACs in particular parliamentary systems.

Accountability is not just designed to catch out its subject in an illegal practice. Of course, one wishes to have control systems that are capable of doing this. But if accountability relied entirely on catching people out it would inevitably fail, short of turning the country into a police state. Accountability is about instilling or reinforcing an ethos of legal compliance and efficient practice. It works by motivating people in ways that are beyond their direct control to engage in desired conduct. At its highest level, if a government is required to answer on the floor of the House for its actions, that is a real incentive for ministers to avoid improper or imprudent actions that are likely to be revealed by parliamentary scrutiny. One needs to be careful in devising and operating motivating factors. For example, unduly bureaucratic controls can become a real inhibition to efficient administrative practice, to the detriment of good government. Furthermore, an unduly rigorous approach to scrutiny can make administrators risk-averse and inhibit them from pursuing new ideas or systems, with the loss of potential pay-offs in better managed operations.

These latter examples are ever-present dangers. Rigorous accountability must be tempered by the consideration that it exists to promote good governance, not as an end in itself. In a PAC context this will require fair judgement and understanding to be brought to bear on administrative practices and initiatives that are under scrutiny before the committee, lest undesirable disincentives to efficient practices are introduced.

PUBLIC ACCOUNTS COMMITTEES AND AUDITORS-GENERAL

A PAC is one organisational form in which Parliament ensures the accountability of government. But for the PAC to function at all it requires the information essential to a proper assessment of the governance and performance issues it wishes to address. In almost all countries this is largely provided by an independent state auditor (referred to in this report as the Auditor-General). It is the Auditor-General's role to help ensure that the use of public sector resources is adequately accounted for by the government, both by the extensive independent audit, and report work carried out by the Auditor-General's office, and by supporting the work of the PAC.

So intertwined is the relationship between the PAC and the Auditor-General that the Study Group found it impossible to confine its remit wholly to the PAC. To have done so would have given an inadequate idea of the parliamentary accountability exercised in regard to the use of public sector resources. The PAC and the Auditor-General are separate organisations, with separate mandates and complementary roles. The exact way in which they work together (and to a greater or lesser extent they do always work together) varies from Parliament to Parliament. There are shared principles of public financial accountability among CPA countries, but there is no common model. Nevertheless, together PACs and Auditors-General are essential components of the democratic accountability which has been outlined above.

These considerations concerning the relationship between Parliament, especially the PAC, and the Auditor-General have led the Study Group to the view that this relationship should be expressed by recognising the Auditor-General as an officer of the Parliament or, where this is more appropriate, of the lower House of the Parliament. Many countries already do this. To emphasise the responsibility of the Auditor-General to Parliament rather than the executive arm of government, the Study Group strongly endorses the principle of independence from the Executive.

STATUS OF PACS AND AUDITORS-GENERAL

Given the importance and nexus of PACs and Auditors-General, the Study Group's report is largely concerned with their accountability functions. This will involve a consideration of the status of both the PAC and the Auditor-General. They in turn are accountable, as is everyone, in the sense that they are subject to motivating factors beyond their control. But are these motivating factors appropriate? In this regard the transparency and method of appointing an Auditor-General needs to be considered, along with the term of office (tenure) and legal position of that officer. These factors help to establish the formal independence (or not) of the office. Alongside them are questions of funding and resources for Auditors-General. These are relevant factors in considering the de facto independence of the office. The formal and practical positions may, of course, differ.

For a PAC, executive/legislative relations are critical. Recent Australian legislation strengthening the role of the PAC and the Auditor-General has been described as an important shift of power from the executive to the legislature. It is now seen as a significant factor on Parliament's side in the balance of power. But even without such a dramatic change as this, matters such as the composition of the committee, whether its Chair is drawn from the government or the opposition ranks, its terms of reference (especially whether or not it has a policy remit), openness of hearings, frequency of meeting and resources (including the quality of audit information provided by the Auditor-General) are factors that help to determine its effectiveness as a check on the exercise of executive power.

THE COST OF ACCOUNTABILITY

Accountability through the PAC and the Auditor-General is not costless. Adequate resources in time and money need to be invested in both organisations if they are to work effectively. It is the Study Group's view, however, that failing to have an appropriate form of PAC and Auditor-General is simply not an option. Good government for both internal and external reasons requires these components. An independent and adequately resourced Auditor-General is essential. In a parliamentary context, it is not appropriate to speak of an 'independent' PAC. The PAC, like all other committees, is responsible to its parent body. It cannot be independent of the House that appointed it. In the case of the PAC, what is needed is a body which can be politically effective rather than independent in a formal sense. How that political effectiveness can be instilled will be discussed later. But apart from this, it is quite clear that a PAC, working more on accountability than policy, needs to be adequately resourced to be able to function effectively.

The 'cost' of democracy or the return on investment, in the sense of a PAC and an Auditor-General carrying out their functions to a high degree of effectiveness, is impossible to quantify. But as an illustration of the benefits to be obtained from setting up effective systems, it has been estimated in Ontario that savings of C$500 million have resulted over an eight year period from implementation of the Auditor-General's recommendations. While it is accepted that such estimates are always tenuous, this is a dramatic illustration of the difference in money terms that such institutions can make. At a basic level the mere presence of the Auditor-General's staff and the existence of a legislative mechanism for holding the executive to account in a public manner is a severe disincentive to defalcation and corruption.

It is difficult to overestimate the importance to accountability and thus to good governance of the PAC and the Auditor-General.

The international dimension

GREATER INTERDEPENDENCY

The concept of the PAC dates back to 1861, when the House of Commons at Westminster established such a committee to consider the reports of the Comptroller and Auditor-General. It is most unlikely that the parliamentarians who established the PAC in the middle of the nineteenth century were at all concerned with international opinion, but the situation today is very different. We are living in an inter-dependent world. Flows of trade, capital and transfer payments across national boundaries are enormous, not just in comparison with Victorian times but even in comparison with those of a few decades ago.

What this means is that as countries our 'neighbours' are all interested in our domestic political and financial infrastructures, and that our 'neighbours' constitute potentially the rest of the world: nation states, international organisations, non-governmental organisations and private investors and donors. Each country's financial standing in the world increasingly depends upon how it is perceived by these growing global constituencies.

CREDITWORTHINESS OF NATIONS

In respect of developing nations seeking overseas development assistance, questions of giving assurances on their domestic political and financial infrastructures as a condition of that assistance are not new. But the imperatives of financial interdependency are not confined to developing nations. Developed nations also wish to attract capital investment that is looking for a financial home throughout the world. Their ability to do so is also partly dependent upon the assurances that they can give to potential investors about the fiduciary framework that exists as an element of good governance within their jurisdictions. This good governance element is an increasingly important factor in determining the creditworthiness of nations.

The interest in establishing strong domestic fiduciary frameworks at the national and sub-national levels is an interest that developing and developed nations have in common, for both depend on the flow of international finance essential to maintaining and enhancing their standards of living. The Study Group has focused particularly on the role of PACs and Auditors-General in helping to provide attestation and assurance on the integrity of financial infrastructures, at least insofar as the public sector is concerned. Any assessment of a country's credit rating should take the existence and operation of these accountability institutions into account.

CHANGING NATURE OF LENDING

The role of the PAC and the Auditor-General as important elements in the financial infrastructure has been enhanced by the changing nature of lending by international financial institutions.

In respect of the World Bank, for example, 50 per cent of its lending is now in the form of adjustment lending or budgetary support, rather than lending for particular investment projects. There is consequently less emphasis than there once was on borrowers satisfying performance conditions in respect of a particular investment loan (for example, targets for building a particular road or factory). Rather than lenders exclusively monitoring how funds are used on individual projects, attention has shifted to how overall resources are utilised and accountability institutions function. National governments rather than international lending institutions then take greater ownership of their own investment projects and decide how adjustment loans are used to finance national requirements.

This means that a strong public financial accounting mechanism that encompasses all of the country's public sector and its management of resources is often the most important consideration to the international lender in regard to governmental development loans. Because international financial assistance is increasingly intermingled with a country's domestic revenues, it is the domestic fiduciary framework that provides attestation and assurance that funds are being used with probity, and efficiently and effectively. Consequently, the attention of international lenders is being up-scaled: shifting from 'project' level to 'country' level accountability and financial management systems and related scrutiny mechanisms. In the public sector this means strong PACs and Auditors-General.

As a result there is now considerable interest on the part of the international community in encouraging capacity building in this area of governance. Nations must be given assistance to develop the audit and other investigatory skills needed to carry out these functions. One potential difficulty is that international financial institutions deal mainly with governments rather than Parliaments. Governments clearly are interested in building such capacities where they perceive a need to give international assurances. Thus the Study Group was told that in Pakistan, where Parliament is in abeyance, the regime has agreed to establish a proto-PAC to carry out the functions that would otherwise be performed by the PAC in a parliamentary environment. Obviously this is not an ideal situation but, given political conditions in Pakistan, it is a good illustration of the way in which governments can come to recognise the importance of having a PAC as an element of good governance and sound public sector accountability.

CONTACT BETWEEN PACS AND INTERNATIONAL LENDERS

Even though governments are showing increasing awareness of the essential role of PACs, it may be that a greater contact should be fostered between Parliaments, through PACs, and international financial institutions, so that there could be a direct exchange of views between them. In this way PACs could learn directly what is of concern to international lenders and how PACs as institutional checks can help to improve domestic performance in the management and use of all public sector resources. Conversely, international lenders can learn how PACs can help them to obtain assurance that the financial resources that they provide, along with those raised from domestic sources, are being used effectively. It is important that international institutions regard Members of Parliament as stakeholders in the development they are helping to foster and that they stress the importance of parliamentary controls. This would help to generate a demand for greater parliamentary accountability.

The Study Group believes that direct contacts on a country by country basis between Parliaments and international lenders would be mutually beneficial.

INTERNATIONAL CORRUPTION

One important issue (beyond the capacity even of PACs in general to deal with) is corruption in international transactions, particularly corruption facilitated by the use of the Internet. This is a global issue. It has profound effects on each nation's revenue stream, since international financial transactions can lead to moneys disappearing from any nation's public accounts. PACs are part of the means of confronting international corruption, but they are not the whole answer. Indeed a major problem in dealing with this issue is that there is no supranational body tasked with addressing it.

In this context the idea of some form of accountability forum needs to be explored. To some extent this is part of building good governance: providing accountability, ensuring transparency and combating corruption. As a start, the Study Group would encourage the CPA to include such good government subjects as themes or sub-themes in its conferences. We were pleased to see, for example, that the 2001 conference included an item on combating corruption. Such matters can be given prominence in the future too.

The Study Group also heard about moves to set up an inter-parliamentary association – Global Parliamentarians Against Corruption (GOPAC) – to provide a forum for individual members to learn about developments in this area. It is hoped that as GOPAC expands its organisation into all regions of the world, it will provide a means whereby individual Members of Parliament can collaborate in the fight against corruption. Related parliamentary organisations such as the Canadian Parliamentary Centre (which will act as the international secretariat for GOPAC) are also involved in organising good governance programmes and seminars that include anti-corruption elements.

Auditors-General

The Study Group spent a considerable part of its time discussing the position of Auditors-General.

The matter of fundamental importance for an Auditor-General is independence. Independence in this sense means independence from the entity being audited, which in the Auditor-General's case means from the government, as it is the government and government-owned entities over which the Auditor-General's remit runs. Independence, of course, has to be reconciled with accountability, because no entity or individual should be unaccountable. Also independence does not mean insulation from the suggestions and persuasions of others. Auditors-General must be sensitive to political and public concerns, and it is perfectly legitimate, indeed essential, that those concerns should be important influences on how Auditors-General distribute their audit resources. The Study Group does not see strong PAC influences on an Auditor-General's work programme as being incompatible with an Auditor-General's independence. Indeed, an Auditor-General's close relationship with the PAC should be used as one means of maintaining the Auditor-General's independence. For example, in Australia, under new legislation, that Parliament's PAC has responsibility for safeguarding the Auditor-General's independence.

Independence has a number of aspects; it is not achieved or guaranteed by one factor. Such matters as the method of appointment, tenure, career expectations, method of removal, funding and legal immunities attaching to the office are all important to an overall assessment of the extent to which an Auditor-General can be said to be independent. Nor are formal rules determinative of this. Indeed how the Auditor-General operates in practice and whether he or she exercises a greater or lesser degree of freedom over the work that is done are more significant than paper guarantees of independence which amount to little because sufficient resources are not provided to enable an adequate job to be done. In this regard, local circumstances and conventions will ultimately be the important ingredients in establishing independence.

However, the Study Group did feel that it was important, regardless of the detailed rules on the matters referred to above, that it be formally established that the Auditor-General is not part of the executive arm of government; that the Auditor-General is not a government auditor. For this reason the association with the legislature as an Officer of Parliament has more than merely symbolic importance. It is an expression of the wholly different standing of an Auditor-General from that of other civil servants who are responsible to the government, which in turn is accountable to Parliament. The Auditor-General should be both responsible and accountable to Parliament, and clearly seen as being located in the legislative branch of government. How this aim might be given effect in practice is discussed in this section.

APPOINTMENT

There is a diverse number of ways in which Auditors-General are appointed, and there is no one 'correct' manner.

Obviously a purely governmental appointment with no outside consultation at all would not be conducive to the independence of the position. But that does not mean that a wholly parliamentary-based process for appointment is essential either. After all, as in most of our parliamentary systems the executive is contained within the legislature, it is wrong to think of the two branches as wholly dichotomous. A parliamentary appointment that consisted of a government majority imposing its choice of Auditor-General on the legislature on political grounds, with no opportunity of consultation with other parties in the House, would be equally as objectionable as a straightforward appointment by the executive made on the same grounds. Making an appointment by parliamentary means does not in itself give the Auditor-General legitimacy in terms of the independence of the office.

So it is important to build a broader base to the way in which the appointment decision is made, rather than to concentrate attention exclusively on who makes it. In Canada appointment is made by Order in Council, but only after receiving nominations from a special committee of audit professionals, including the Institute of Chartered Accountants. The Chair of the PAC is also consulted prior to the final decision being made. In Australia the Joint Committee on Public Accounts and Audit can conduct public hearings on the executive's nominee for appointment, and can exercise a veto over that appointment. In the United Kingdom we understand that the practice is for the Prime Minister to nominate the person to be appointed, with the agreement of the Chair of the PAC.

What is important is an appointment process that leads to confidence that the appointee will be able to carry out the duties of office independently. The specific details of who actually makes the appointment are a subsidiary matter. But the determination of the person who is to be appointed should involve more than just the government. A wider range of stakeholder interests other than purely government interests must be represented (such as opposition parties, PACs and other audit specialists) in a way that allows them to make a genuine contribution to the final decision.

The Study Group also discussed the field from which an Auditor-General might be appointed. In this regard it was concerned not to cut off any avenues for appointment. The position of Auditor-General is one of the great offices of state. It may not always be possible to fill it from the career civil servants who are working in the Auditor-General's office. It is quite appropriate that an outside person of distinction may be appointed to the position, especially when that person has special skills that may be necessary to the future direction in which Parliament desires that the office should develop. But the group was also concerned that nothing should be done to undermine the career aspirations of those auditors who have spent their working lives as civil service auditors. They also must be able to aspire realistically to the position of Auditor-General, and the appointment process must give them a reasonable opportunity of appointment.

TERM OF OFFICE

An important component of an Auditor-General's independence is the term of office to which he or she is appointed. A very short-term appointment to office would hardly give the Auditor-General the confidence to exercise the powers of the office in a way that was uninfluenced by considerations of the effects on one's future career.

A number of terms of office are in effect throughout the world. In Canada and Australia the terms are ten years. The group understands that the United States has a 15-year term. On the other hand, Singapore formerly made the appointment for the remainder of the office-holder's career, effectively a life-time appointment, though it has more recently reduced this to a fixed-term appointment. For smaller countries affordability is a concern with fixed-term appointments that lead to a succession of holders of the office, since each holder of the office is entitled to an individual remuneration package and pension, and a number of such persons can be relatively expensive for a country with a small revenue base.

Overall, the Study Group felt that the independence of the office flows more from the manner of appointment and the funding of the office rather than its term.

RENEWABILITY OF TERM

An associated issue is whether an Auditor-General's term can be renewed when it comes to an end. Some countries with relatively long fixed terms, such as the United States, Australia and Canada, forbid reappointment of the Auditor-General. Others have no rule on the matter. On the one hand, the possibility of a renewal of one's term clearly could affect the Auditor-General's approach to the position in ways that are undesirable. On the other hand, quality audit skills are not so abundant that all countries can afford to dispense with an Auditor-General's services when that appointee's term expires.

If the possibility of being reappointed led the Auditor-General to favour those responsible for the reappointment or with the greatest influence over it, this would be improper. However, such a development is best addressed by constructing a robust appointments process that removes the incentive to curry favour with any one group involved in making the appointment. Appointment as Auditor-General might not occur close to one's normal retirement age, and the Auditor-General may still be vigorous and capable of leading the state's audit team. Developing countries particularly cannot afford to be profligate in discarding talented people. Consequently, it was felt by the group that there could be no absolute objection in all circumstances to renewal. Whether a term was open to renewal would depend upon conditions in each country and the length of the initial term of appointment with, in the case of relatively short-term appointments, a presumption that renewal would be available.

A related issue is whether an Auditor-General, after leaving office, should be able to hold an office of profit under the Crown or whether, at least for a period, such an appointment should not be open to a former Auditor-General. Given the development of such restrictions for former ministers, it is not inappropriate that consideration be given to developing similar restrictions for Auditors-General and other senior civil servants who have recently left office.

REMOVAL FROM OFFICE

As part of the accountability of an Auditor-General there must be a process for removing or suspending the occupant from office before the expiration of his or her term. But clearly this possibility must be very circumscribed.

A common removal method is by the Parliament on certain stated grounds. This method often corresponds to the procedure for the removal of a judge. Certainly the Study Group saw it as being essential that removal only be possible on grounds that are defined in advance by the law. This is an essential part of the independence of the Auditor-General. It would undermine that independence if an Auditor-General were removable simply because a government had changed and the new majority in the House wished to substitute a political appointee of its own. Common grounds that have been defined as giving cause for removing an Auditor-General from office include conviction of crime, bankruptcy, insanity or other inability to carry out the functions of office. Any provision for removing an Auditor-General from office should be confined to reasons (however defined) such as these.

As has been stated, the actual removal decision is usually left to Parliament, and this is appropriate. The group noted that in Singapore, removal is effected as part of the judicial process rather than by the executive or the legislature. Even in those countries that repose the removal power in the executive or the legislature, it may well be that the judiciary could still have a role to play if it was asked to review whether as a matter of law the grounds for removing an Auditor-General actually existed. This would seem to be a distinct possibility where the removal process is part of a constitutional guarantee of Auditor-General independence.

RECRUITMENT AND TRAINING OF STAFF

An Auditor-General needs the right to appoint staff, since no Auditor-General can carry out the duties of the office alone. This raises the question of the ability to recruit staff and determine their terms and conditions of employment.

In many countries the permanent staff of an Auditor-General's office are civil servants who are likely to be recruited by means that are similar to those for the recruitment of civil servants generally in the particular country concerned. (In the United Kingdom such staff are no longer classified as civil servants.) Many staff will have been recruited from other parts of the public service itself. However, the wider scope of the audit tasks being undertaken today (such as performance audits and environmental audits) mean that inevitably Auditors-General need staff with a wider range of skills than has been traditional in the past. Staff with non-auditor qualifications can be recruited into the Auditor-General's office on a permanent basis to provide these skills, and they can be supplemented by engagements of staff for a short period or for a particular project where they have special skills that are needed by the Auditor-General. The resources allocated to the Auditor-General's office will determine whether the Auditor-General is able to make such appointments and whether sufficient numbers of staff with appropriate skills can be recruited.

A further source of staff resources is by secondment from other parts of the public service. Different Auditors-General may follow different policies on their links with the public service at large. The Study Group heard that in Canada there is considerable interchange between the Auditor-General's office and the public service, and that the Auditor-General's staff can be seconded for up to two years to public service departments. Staff are seconded from departments to the Canadian Auditor-General's office too, though movement this way is not so extensive as secondments to departments. On the other hand, exchanges of this nature with the public service are infrequent in Ontario.

The Study Group sees value in secondment as a means of developing staff by increasing their range of experiences. Secondment to a public service department will help auditors to see problems from an internal perspective. This should enable them to understand better the problems of entities which they are auditing, and make them more effective auditors. However, there is a feeling that an auditor could be compromised in effectiveness by a lengthy secondment if it led to that officer taking a less than dispassionate view of departmental problems. The Study Group certainly agrees that an auditor should not audit an entity to which the auditor had been seconded. But it does see secondment, both to the public and to the private sectors, as a desirable practice that will help to develop staff skills in Auditors-General's offices.

TRAINING FOR AUDITORS-GENERAL

Training for an Auditor-General himself or herself is a more problematic matter. To be appointed as Auditor-General the person concerned will already have achieved a professional standing that will have involved considerable training. Yet one should not ignore the fact that as Auditor-General the individual is taking on new and onerous responsibilities, and support for that task must be provided. The Study Group felt that international Auditors-General associations have an important role to play in this regard. Through these associations Auditors-General can learn from the experiences of colleagues who have faced similar problems. Rather than a training role, newly-appointed Auditors-General can benefit from the mentoring effect of interaction with their peers. Through international associations too, invaluable information about the latest developments in the field can be exchanged, thus helping to keep Auditors-General up to date with the state of the art in public sector auditing. Indeed, it is in such forums that the state of the art is defined.

The Study Group therefore endorses active participation in such associations by Auditors-General.

AUDITORS-GENERAL'S RELATIONSHIPS

Executive

The Study Group has already given its reasons for considering that the Auditor-General should not be a part of the executive.

The Auditor-General must be independent in the discharge of all aspects of the role, and the Auditor-General and the Auditor-General's staff must approach their task of auditing government as external auditors. But necessarily the Auditor-General's relationship with the executive is more ongoing than merely one of conducting an annual external audit of the Public Accounts.

First, as has already been discussed, the executive will almost certainly be involved in the appointment process. As the executive is a leading, indeed often a dominant, component of a parliamentary system of government, this is inevitable, and is not necessarily incompatible with an Auditor-General's independence. But for the reasons given above, conventions or rules that ensure transparency and consensus over such appointments are critical in ensuring the degree of independence for the Auditor-General that we see as necessary.

Second, the Auditor-General's staff may be part of the regular civil service, and in administering the office the Auditor-General is likely to be subject to the constraints operating on other departmental heads within the public service. This leads to questions of how the Auditor-General's office should be resourced. (This issue is discussed below: see pp. 43–4.)

Third, the Auditor-General is not discharging his or her functions on a contractual basis with the entities being audited, as is a private sector auditor. It may well be that in some countries payments are made to the Auditor-General for audit services by the entities being audited. Organising an Auditor-General's office into a business unit that seeks to recover costs is a means of promoting efficiency in its operations. But even where this is done the relationship is not a commercial one. The Auditor-General is discharging a public duty, and that public duty overrides any other interest that may arise. The department is not a client in a business sense who chooses to use a particular audit firm. The department is subject to the Auditor-General's audit as an inescapable consequence of being part of the public sector. Nevertheless, instilling something akin to a provider/client relationship that is given monetary expression is important where outsourcing of audit work takes place. (This is discussed below: see pp. 48–51.)

For these reasons a good working relationship with the executive is important, so that an Auditor-General has easy access to it and relates comfortably to senior officials. The concept of independence should not make an Auditor-General's office aloof from the public service, nor encourage it to set out to embarrass the executive. While the Auditor-General should always retain the right to speak out critically in public if necessary, in the main the relationship should be one of harmonious coexistence, not competition. The Study Group believes too that the Auditor-General has a role in allowing the executive to manage its response to the Auditor-General's reports by, in suitable cases, briefing it in advance of the release of a report, so that an informed response is capable of being made to a report that requires an immediate reaction on the part of the government. In this way a positive relationship with the executive can be promoted.

Legislature

The Study Group considers that Auditors-General should have the status of Officers of Parliament. This means that the Auditor-General is responsible to and reports to the legislature as a whole. The Auditor-General should not be regarded as an official of a single committee, even the PAC. Indeed, we envisage the Auditor-General potentially having a working relationship with every committee of the legislature, if the Auditor-General can provide expertise that is relevant to the work of those committees. It would therefore be unfortunate if Auditors-General did not look beyond PACs for means of relating to legislatures, or if PACs tried to constrain the provision of Auditors-General assistance to other committees. However, the ability to reach out to the work of other committees in this way will depend upon resources, and it must not be at the cost of an effective working relationship with PACs.

Subject to the resources to realise this potential, Auditors-General should take active steps to introduce themselves and their offices to all members and all committees. Briefing members after each election (either by participating in induction courses which other parliamentary authorities organise or through programmes they arrange themselves) is one method of promoting their availability. Personally contacting the chairpersons of committees after their appointment or election and arranging more detailed briefings for each committee would also be appropriate. Establishing a relationship with the staff who service committees can also be an effective way of promoting the Auditor-General's office's services to committees. The Canadian Auditor-General's office has established a small group within the office responsible for relationships with parliamentarians. Whether an Auditor-General has the resources to do this or not, it is desirable that Auditors-General think about developing a whole-of-legislature relationship.

Public Accounts Committees

While an Auditor-General may be an Officer of Parliament, it is inevitable that the relationship with the legislature tends to find its principal form of expression in the Auditor-General's relationship with the PAC. This is both because historically PACs were created to ensure parliamentary follow-up on Auditors-General's reports, and because the jurisdiction of PACs has more in common with Auditors-General's remits than does that of other committees.

However, the relationship between the Auditor-General and the PAC is by no means uniform. It has evolved differently in different jurisdictions. One can postulate something of a continuum, from no apparent contact at all between Auditors-General and PACs, to a relationship that is almost exclusively reciprocal between the Auditor-General and the PAC, with the Auditor-General reporting solely to the PAC, and the PAC relying exclusively on the Auditor-General's report as a source for its inquiries.

In Australia a parliamentary committee's report led to legislation designed to give meaning to the Auditor-General's relationship with Parliament. One of its outcomes was the establishment of a committee which provides the Auditor-General with a principal point of entry to Parliament. In the United Kingdom the chairman of the PAC participates in the process of appointing an Auditor-General. In general, regardless of the closeness of the relationship, one would expect that the principal way in which expression is given to the Auditor-General's position as an Officer of Parliament is the working relationship with the PAC. This can involve providing the PAC with material that forms the basis of its inquiry work, assisting the committee to carry out that work, and in turn receiving suggestions from the PAC as to the work programme that the Auditor-General may undertake. For example, in India the relationship between the PAC and the Auditor-General is extremely close in all aspects of the committee's work, and in Canada at least 95 per cent of the PAC's time is spent considering the Auditor-General's reports. (This relationship is examined further on pp. 58–9.)

Working practices

How the relationship may work in practice can be usefully examined by contrasting two Canadian jurisdictions – the province of Ontario and Canada itself – where there are marked differences in the way that the PAC and the Auditor-General work together.

In Ontario the PAC may by resolution refer matters to the Auditor-General for report. Such matters must then be reported on by the Auditor-General. The PAC itself has a very close working relationship with the Auditor-General. The Auditor-General briefs the PAC in private. At public examinations of witnesses, the Auditor-General sits with the Chair of the PAC and participates in the hearings by questioning witnesses with the Chair's permission. The Auditor-General then helps the PAC in the drafting of its report on the matter under inquiry. In Ontario the PAC usually endorses the Auditor-General's reports and recommendations.

In Canada the relationship between the PAC and the Auditor-General, while cordial, is more arms-length. All the Auditor-General's reports stand referred to the PAC. But at PAC hearings on those reports, the Auditor-General appears and gives evidence as a witness, not as a member of the committee's staff. In fact, the PAC does not automatically hear from the Auditor-General on every inquiry that it initiates. In 2000 the Auditor-General appeared before the PAC as a witness at 22 of its 31 meetings (most of the remaining meetings were dedicated to preparing its reports). The Auditor-General contributes to the PAC's conclusions through the evidence he or she provides to the committee, but does not assist in framing those conclusions by participating in the drafting of PAC reports.

Ontario and Canada illustrate quite different relationships between the Auditor-General and the PAC with, on the one hand, the Auditor-General being the committee's principal adviser while, on the other, the Auditor-General is the committee's principal witness. For other PACs the Auditor-General's relationship with the PAC may more often take on aspects of both roles at different points in the process. In the United Kingdom, for example, the Auditor-General gives evidence to the PAC as a witness, but the Auditor-General or the Auditor-General's staff are also present when the committee deliberates on its reports.

The Study Group does not see any preferred model for the PAC/Auditor-General working relationship. But it is important that the conceptual differences between the Auditor-General as a witness and the Auditor-General as an adviser be appreciated. In particular, evidence given to any tribunal must be subject to examination and testing as to its accuracy, and to submission from others as to what conclusions are to be drawn from it. Evidence from Auditors-General is no different in this respect. It too must be available for any person with an interest in the matter to comment on and to attempt to refute if the person feels so inclined. An adviser to a committee helps the committee to interpret and manage the evidence it has heard, but an adviser should not create new evidence that has not been subjected to this testing process. An Auditor-General who is both a witness and an adviser must keep these roles distinct so as not to create an impression of unfairness on the part of persons affected by the PAC's inquiries and reports.

THE ROLE OF THE AUDITOR-GENERAL

Standards

The increasing internationalisation of public sector accounting and audit leads inevitably to the question of defining acceptable standards across audit jurisdictions. The ability to make realistic comparisons of performance in this area is of even greater importance in a globalised world.

The number of private audit firms operating at an international level is reducing, but the Study Group did not see private firms as being responsible for establishing standards in any case. International bodies are attempting to promulgate international audit standards that may gain wide acceptance; however, the difficulty with such standards is that their application at the national level can differ significantly. The expertise in legislative audit lies with Auditor-General, and it is Auditors-General, with the support of PACs, who we see establishing internationally-recognised public audit standards and practices. Standards should be prescribed in detail, not just left to the skill and judgement of auditors to develop.

While the establishment of agreed standards is essential, the major difficulty faced by developing nations is building the capacity to achieve them. Developing capacity in this field is a major challenge.

In regard to standards, the Study Group noted that there was disquiet at the competition within the shrinking number of international firms to win audit assignments, and the effect that this could have on their diligence in carrying out their work. An auditor who is worried about losing an audit contract would be less likely to probe deeply and ask difficult questions of those directing the entity being audited. A number of prominent international failures have left auditors with expensive legal actions launched against them by liquidators and creditors. Steps have also been taken by public bodies, such as the Securities and Exchange Commission in the United States, to discourage auditors buying stock in companies that they audit. Another issue with private auditors is the use of consulting arms of audit firms as loss-leaders to help them obtain the more lucrative audit work. Moves have been made to restrict auditors from engaging in consultancies for their audit clients, and in some prominent cases the consulting arm of audit firms has been devolved to a separate firm.

Auditors-General with a legislative mandate do not have these problems of client control or conflict of interest. Their clients are Parliaments and PACs, not the entity being audited, and they do not run consulting arms. Auditors-General may utilise the services of private firms to help them to carry out their audit mandates should the Auditor-General's office not have the resources to carry out all of the work in-house. Indeed it is not necessarily desirable that everything be accomplished in-house. But even where private firms are employed to carry out public sector audits, they are doing so under the direction of the Auditor-General and are subject to the established public audit standards. We hope in the future that those public audit standards will have an international currency.

Internal audit

The Auditor-General is the external auditor of public sector agencies. Internal audit is part of a management responsibility to maintain, on a day to day basis, effective systems that ensure that financial transactions comply with the law or other applicable financial authorities. Internal audit is part of a system of controls that enable management to assess and control risks faced by the entity concerned.

As part of the external audit, the Auditor-General will make an assessment of the effectiveness of the internal audit, though the responsibility for it resides with the management of the department or agency concerned.

The Study Group sees it as essential that internal audit standards be prescribed just as external audit standards need to be prescribed. These standards in many cases are in practice set by a central government agency, such as the Treasury, which has financial control over all departments. But ideally internal audit standards should receive endorsement from an agency outside the governmental structure, such as the Auditor-General. In Canada a special body – the Public Sector Accounting Board of the Canadian Institute of Chartered Accountants – sets such standards. The Auditor-General is a member of the Board. An arms-length approach to setting standards is to be preferred.

Performance evaluation

The public sector traditionally reported in its financial statements the revenues collected under authority granted by Parliament and the expenditure of resources appropriated to it by Parliament. The Auditor-General's audit was to ensure on a test basis that these statements fairly represented the financial transactions of the government, that public money and stores were properly accounted for, and that appropriated funds had been expended only for the purposes of the parliamentary appropriation. Audit was concerned with probity and compliance. The results of these financial transactions were beyond the Auditor-General's remit.

However, in recent decades there have been demands to know more about performance and results, rather than merely accounting for legality and propriety in public expenditure. Consequently, and paralleling developments in public sector financial management generally, the role of public audit has expanded from a concentration on the inputs used by the public sector to a concern with what governments are actually producing – their outputs. In audit terms this concern is not so much with whether those outputs are desirable in themselves (though in extreme cases this question could be raised) but with whether the outputs are being produced as efficiently as possible with the least cost to public funds, and whether they are delivering their anticipated benefits. In sum, is the public receiving 'value for money' in respect of its investment? In the effort to answer these questions, other issues inescapably arise. It becomes more necessary for public sector managers to define in advance of embarking on a programme precisely what that programme is expected to achieve and, in order to measure whether it has actually achieved those results, to devise standards against which its performance can be measured.

Thus a whole range of management tools for ensuring good public sector performance has come into existence, through the shift of emphasis from a focus on inputs and a process-based accountability, to a focus on outputs and a results-based accountability.

Auditors-General began to move in the direction of performance audits in the 1970s. This type of work now occupies the majority of the audit time in developed countries: 75 per cent of the Auditor-General's work in the United Kingdom involves value for money audits, 67 per cent of the Canadian Auditor-General's audit effort. Moreover in those countries it is the performance audit reports that parliamentarians and the public primarily identify with. Compliance auditing tends to be routine and relatively dull, except in the rare instance of a major defalcation being exposed.

On the other hand, performance-based audit is more resource intensive. It can take considerable time, and requires a wide range of skills going well beyond those of the traditional auditor. In Ontario it has been necessary almost to halve the number of performance-based audits carried out compared with a decade ago, because of a lack of resources for the Auditor-General's office.

This change of audit focus has altered the perception of the Auditor-General's role. The role has expanded from being an auditor of the public accounts and financial transactions of the state to that of a promoter of organisational performance. In some countries value for money auditing has now been recognised within the Auditor-General's legislative mandate, though it is only the delivery of the programme that is audited. The political raison d'être for the programme's existence is beyond the mandate of the Auditor-General's examination. The United Kingdom legislation recognises this distinction by stating that the Auditor-General is not to question the merits of the policy objectives of the department or body concerned. This, whether enshrined in statute or not, is an essential element in the conventions under which Auditors-General work.

The objectives of performance-based auditing are often expressed in terms of economy, efficiency and effectiveness. Economy involves minimising the use of public resources; efficiency is concerned with the achievement of the objects of the programme with the least use of resources; effectiveness is concerned with establishing whether intended results were actually achieved.

In contrast to compliance auditing, where it is usually possible to reach objective conclusions on matters, performance auditing is inherently subjective. It is much more judgemental than traditional auditing. One way of minimising this subjectivity is to agree on well-defined performance standards in advance. Much audit effort is therefore focused on forcing departments to define what they expect to achieve, and expressing this in firm performance standards which can be measured.

Performance-based auditing by the Auditor-General motivates departments to improve their operational performance and delivery of goods and services. The Auditor-General is part of the accountability process which promotes greater public sector productivity. But it must be conceded that the advent of performance-based auditing increases the likelihood of conflict between Auditors-General and departments, through the potential for disagreements over the judgements that are involved at all stages. Nevertheless, it is an essential aspect of the work of an Auditor-General. For those Auditors-General who are still primarily concerned with compliance auditing, value for money auditing is likely to grow considerably more important in the future, not least as a result of international pressures for countries to put in place an infrastructure that promotes good public sector performance. Performance-based auditing challenges departments to justify not just what they are spending, but also what they are producing. It can therefore raise fundamentally important questions about how the public sector is organised.

Environmental and gender impact auditing

Auditing the public sector today is undoubtedly much broader in scope than merely examining financial statements. In particular, some Auditors-General are auditing programmes for their environmental and gender impacts. In some cases this expansion of the Auditor-General's mandate has been legislatively mandated. Thus in Canada the Auditor-General is statutorily required to report on whether departments have met their sustainable development objectives and strategies. A Commissioner for the Environment as part of the Auditor-General's office has been established for this purpose. Other countries have chosen to establish a Commissioner for the Environment as a separate office from the Auditor-General and assigned a more policy-oriented role.

While it is accepted that there is an increasing expectation that Auditors-General should conduct audits and report on environmental and gender issues, it is important that this be done as part of the regular examination of programme effectiveness, without Auditors-General trespassing into areas of policy judgement or arrogating to themselves a role which Auditors-General have no particular expertise to perform. Auditors-General can however seek to establish whether there are governmental systems in place to measure the effectiveness of environmental or gender programmes. Without imposing their own views on the effectiveness of such programmes, Auditors-General will also be legitimately interested in the performance measures that governments develop for this purpose. Furthermore, Auditors-General can encourage governments to develop their own performance reports, and can as part of the audit role seek to verify the worth of these – establishing, on analogy with traditional audit principles, whether they fairly present the performance of departments and the programmes delivered. The final judgement on the effectiveness of such programmes is a political one to be taken by politicians or the public. But the Auditor-General has an important part to play in ensuring that the information necessary to make such a judgement has been developed and presented.

The Study Group recognises that by expanding their roles on environmental and gender issues, Auditors-General and PACs do run a risk of compromising their political integrity by entering into the area of policy judgement. They are also subject to the criticism that they have no special expertise in these areas arising from their main functions, and should leave the field to other bodies better equipped to deal with them. For these reasons Auditors-General and PACs must move cautiously and confine themselves to laying the groundwork for effectiveness evaluations by others, subject to any statutory mandate that may have been imposed on Auditors-General to make effectiveness judgements themselves.

Budget reporting

The Auditor-General's role in respect of reporting on a government's budget is necessarily more limited than in regard to the Public Accounts. Budgets involve questions of macroeconomic policy, and highly contentious political judgements are involved in assessing them. These are not matters with which an Auditor-General should ordinarily be involved. It is not the role of the Auditor-General as it has hitherto been understood to become an alternative economic adviser to the Parliament. It is for Parliaments to define their own roles in respect of the consideration of the government's budget – for example, whether that role is confined to endorsing the budget as a total package, whether Parliament can amend the budget, or whether Parliament should be more actively involved in framing budgets and allocating resources to particular sectors. Once Parliament's role has been defined, decisions can be made on the resources required by Parliament (such as the Congressional Budget Office in the United States) in order to fulfil its functions. In the meantime the Auditor-General's role is likely to be confined to commenting on the quality of the information used by the government in devising the budget, rather than on the proposals contained in it themselves.

Central bank auditing

There has sometimes been a tendency for the central bank to be exempted from the Auditor-General's remit. The Study Group can see no reason for this. Central banks are part of the public sector like any other agency. They are increasingly being given independence from political direction in setting interest rates and, of course, it is no business of an Auditor-General to second-guess such decisions. But central banks often carry out a range of other functions, such as prudential supervision of the banking sector and open-market operations on behalf of the Treasury. Their performance of these functions should be open to scrutiny by the Auditor-General in the same way as any other public sector agency is expected to account for its performance.

CHOOSING A WORK PROGRAMME

Audit independence

One indication of independence is the freedom to choose what, when and how to audit. Of course, this formal freedom may itself be limited in practice by resource constraints. However, it is important at the outset to make one absolute point: no Auditor-General should be prohibited from inquiring into a matter within the Auditor-General's audit mandate. Auditors-General may receive suggestions from the PAC, other Members of Parliament, or the public on profitable areas of study. The Auditor-General may or may not agree with these suggestions. In some circumstances the Auditor-General may, by law, be required to comply with the suggestions. We see nothing untoward in this. But if the Auditor-General could be prevented from inquiring into a matter which the Auditor-General considered should be inquired into and which fell within the previously defined audit mandate, that would be a recipe for allowing corruption and malpractice. Subject to this, the Auditor-General should be prepared to receive and consider suggestions as to the annual work programme. Making suggestions to an Auditor-General does not compromise his or her audit independence.

Legislative influence

In some cases the legislature or the PAC may be empowered to direct the Auditor-General to inquire into a particular matter. This is the case in Ontario, for example, where the PAC can refer matters to the Auditor-General for report. That is a useful power for a PAC to possess provided that the Auditor-General is not overloaded with mandatory audit referrals that effectively crowd out discretionary audits that the Auditor-General might otherwise wish to undertake. Some legislative direction of an Auditor-General's work is acceptable. Indeed almost every country gives a standing legislative direction to the Auditor-General to examine the Public Accounts; this is the staple of an Auditor-General's work. But legislative direction of a work programme should not amount to the greater portion of an Auditor-General's work, otherwise the Auditor-General's independence and effectiveness may be compromised.

In most countries PACs will have some input into forward audit programmes by reviewing the Auditor-General's proposed programme. In Australia there is an extensive parliamentary involvement in such planning. The PAC seeks the advice of the chairs of all other committees on their preferences for performance reviews, and takes these into account in framing a planned scrutiny strategy for discussion with the Auditor-General. But this parliamentary involvement is predicated on the fact that the Auditor-General has an audit independence which includes freedom to determine the audit programme and the nature and scope of the audits to be conducted. The PAC's suggestions are usually all incorporated into the Auditor-General's work programme.

It is quite common for Auditors-General to have complete discretion as to their work programmes while taking account of PAC preferences and suggestions in framing those programmes. This seems to be the ideal arrangement. Indeed the difficulty for Auditors-General may be too little feedback from members on their audit preferences rather than too much, since members have other preoccupations which can limit meaningful discussions on setting priorities. This is especially the case given that most members are policy-oriented in their interests rather than programme-oriented.

Risk assessment

In terms of developing work programmes, corporate plans with key results areas can give an agreed framework within which operational plans are made. In particular, attempts are being made by Auditors-General to assess risk factors as guides to where audit resources should be deployed. These risk factors include risk of errors in financial results, risk of non-compliance with applicable legal authorities and risk of failure to accomplish the entity's key objectives. When higher risk factors are identified it is worthwhile devoting audit resources to these areas to assist in fixing problems that will inevitably have an impact on satisfactory programme delivery. As well as using risk assessment for more informed guidance of Auditors-General's work programmes, there may also be value in introducing random audits as factors in departmental thinking, so that the potential for close attention from the Auditor-General is always present as a motivator to good practice.

BUDGET AND RESOURCES

Critical to the effective performance of the Auditor-General's functions are the budget and resources provided for the office. The increasing complexity of the modern audit function demands multi-disciplinary audit teams with the need for a range of expertise: legal, economic, environmental and so on. The days when only accountants were employed on public sector audit work are gone. Autonomy of operation depends heavily on sufficiency of resource.

It is in fixing the Auditor-General's budget that reality rather than form is important. The Study Group heard that apparently robust procedures for funding Auditors-General do not necessarily deliver the goods. As with the appointments process, satisfactory outcomes depend very much on the conventions that are developed concerning the funding of Auditors-General's offices, and reliance cannot be placed wholly on paper guarantees.

Parliaments are increasingly developing a pre-budget involvement in fixing the Auditor-General's budget allocation. The PAC may be briefed by the Auditor-General and by the Treasury or Finance Ministry before the government's annual budget is drawn up. This gives the PAC or Parliament an opportunity to recommend the funding to be provided for the Auditor-General before the government's estimates are presented to Parliament. If a convention can be developed, the government would be expected to include this recommended funding in its estimates without alteration. In Australia such recommended funding has the added protection of being legally guaranteed. In the United Kingdom a non-parliamentary body, the Public Audit Commission, of which the Chair of the PAC is a member, performs this function. In other countries the Auditor-General's budget is negotiated through the ordinary estimates process, with no direct parliamentary involvement at the pre-budget stage.

There is no necessary correspondence between these different procedures and an outcome that is satisfactory to Auditors-General in terms of adequate funding. Parliamentary allocation of funding can, with a government majority being brought to bear, result in a squeezing of funding, necessitating staff cuts while the audit domain is growing. The Auditor-General always has the right to report to Parliament, drawing attention to the inadequacy of his or her resources, but this is likely to be of no consolation and have little effect if it was Parliament that took the funding decisions in the first place.

On balance, the Study Group supports parliamentary involvement at the pre-budget stage through the PAC or another parliamentary committee as tending to produce a better funding outcome for Auditors-General. But members must assume responsibility and take an interest themselves in ensuring that Auditors-General have sufficient resources to do the work that is entrusted to them. Capacity for pre-budget involvement of the PAC will not be enough on its own without members taking an interest in safeguarding the role of the Auditor-General from being inhibited due to a lack of resources.

IT developments

The explosion of information technology (IT) has important implications for the way in which Auditors-General carry out their functions. While their auditing objectives do not change, their auditing techniques do. The ways in which organisations now carry on business have changed radically through IT. Auditors-General must focus computer auditing on the risk of irregularities and fraud through electronic transactions, and the rise of e-commerce. Auditors-General have an important role to play in assessing how information systems are integrated into an organisation and managed, particularly from the point of view of the safety and integrity of the system. IT brings enormous benefits but it also brings enormous costs and risks. To perform adequately in this area Auditors-General need their own computing resources and expertise. A considerable and growing effort needs to be put into this area of activity.

LEGAL POWERS AND IMMUNITIES

It is clear that Auditors-General need unrestricted access to the information relevant to the performance of their audit functions.

Normally this will be provided on request by the entity being audited. Indeed a co-operative approach to public sector audit is to be encouraged, with both the Auditor-General and the audit entity having uppermost in their minds the public interest and the contribution that an effective audit service can make to improving outputs. However, behind this normal working relationship it is clear that Auditors-General need the legal powers to require production of documents in exceptional cases.

Many Auditors-General have power to surcharge members and officials in certain circumstances. In France we understand that the PAC has this power. The power to impose a surcharge is a very draconian power to confer on a single officer, even one of the status of an Auditor-General. Its use is very likely to provoke legal challenge directed to both the process followed by the Auditor-General in deciding to impose a surcharge and the judgement made by the Auditor-General that a surcharge was warranted. In the United Kingdom an attempt to impose surcharges on members and officials of a local authority has recently led to over a decade's worth of litigation. The Study Group was not convinced that the power to surcharge was a necessary incident of an Auditor-General's powers. If public funds have been dealt with fraudulently, the criminal law provides a remedy. If they have been applied negligently, civil proceedings to recover losses may be appropriate, perhaps initiated by the Auditor-General. But it is very difficult to justify the Auditor-General being both prosecutor and judge in the matter. Power to impose a surcharge cuts across both of those roles.

The Auditor-General and the Auditor-General's staff do require some legal protections against legal liability that might otherwise be incurred in carrying out their duties. Otherwise it might be too easy to stymie audit investigations by legal action.

Even though an Auditor-General may be an Officer of Parliament, this would not in itself confer any legal protection in respect of audit work carried out outside Parliament. (Obviously reports to Parliament and work carried out on behalf of the PAC would carry the protections flowing from parliamentary proceedings.)

Some legal protections short of absolute immunity would be necessary in respect of this activity. This is regarded as particularly important in developing countries where, to counteract corruption and fraud, there may be a heavy reliance on the inspection functions performed by the Auditor-General's staff. It is important that in carrying out these inspections the staff have legally recognised protections. It is better that these should be defined in the audit legislation than left to be implied.

EXTENT OF THE AUDITOR-GENERAL'S REMIT

Over the last few decades there have been considerable changes in the role of central governments within each nation's economy. In many instances governments have withdrawn from the provision of a number of services that were formerly publicly owned and provided. This has resulted in extensive privatisations of enterprises and services. In other cases the organisational mode of public service delivery has changed either by converting a publicly owned entity into a business unit that tries to operate on more commercial lines (corporatisation) or by contracting service-delivery operations to a private sector organisation while retaining an ultimate public responsibility for the provision of the service. All of these developments pose challenges for public sector audit.

Privatisation

In the case of privatisation, the Auditor-General clearly ceases to be the auditor of the organisation once it has been fully privatised. But the Auditor-General does retain a role in reporting on the process followed in effecting the privatisation and whether this complies with the principles of economy, efficiency and effectiveness. This can pose problems for an Auditor-General who may appear to be questioning a government's policy decision to embark upon a programme of disposal of state undertakings.

However, it is clearly the duty of an Auditor-General to audit the privatisation process to ensure that inefficient choices about the methods by which privatisation is effected are revealed and that the public's interest in obtaining fair value for public assets that are sold, is protected.

Government's shareholding interests

As an alternative to full privatisation the government may maintain an equity interest in a company. This could be a majority or a minority interest. Where the company is not performing a public function, such a government interest is purely adventitious. The Auditor-General, as the auditor of the public estate, may be interested in commenting on the government's investment decision to retain the equity interest, but if there is no public function being performed by the company the auditing mandate of the Auditor-General would not go beyond this.

On the other hand, it is likely that a government's equity interest in a company exists because the company is performing some residual public function. It may also be receiving a public subsidy in addition to the capital investment. The performance of the company may then be a matter of public interest going beyond the investment interest, and the Auditor-General does have a role in elucidating it. In these circumstances the Auditor-General may have the right to concur in the appointment by the company of a private sector auditor, and also have independent rights of access to information from the company and from the auditor's work. The Auditor-General's interest is to ensure that any regulatory and compliance issues have been observed in the performance of public functions and the use of public funds, and also to be satisfied as to the quality of the audit work. Private sector auditors are often reluctant to report on the performance of any community service obligations that attach to a public function or to a government-owned company. Indeed they may have no particular expertise to do so. It is a particular interest of the Auditor-General to ensure that such reporting does occur.

CORPORATISATION AND SERVICE DELIVERY

Corporatisation and contracting for service delivery raise ongoing questions about the Auditor-General's audit mandate. It may well be that one of the consequences of such organisational changes intended by governments and by the new agencies themselves is the attainment of greater freedom from public sector audit. Especially with contractual arrangements, but also potentially through corporatisation, the accountability focus can shift to the relationship between the government and the third party providers, rather than being directly focused on the minister or government department involved. This does pose a challenge to traditional public accountability and scrutiny.

It may be argued from this, for example, that any residual role of the Auditor-General is restricted to examining the adequacy or effectiveness of the relationship – the statement of service performance or the service contract, for instance – rather than on examining the delivery of the service and the entity's performance itself. In more extreme cases there may even be attempts to exclude the Auditor-General's mandate altogether. With corporatised entities a variation on the restrictions to the audit mandate which can occur is a restriction of the Auditor-General's role to that of a private sector auditor performing a general companies legislation audit. In such a case the corporatised entity is not subject to audit based on public sector principles at all, even though the Auditor-General may technically still be the entity's auditor.

One problem with potential reductions in the Auditor-General's mandate when these outsourcing arrangements are being considered is that the PAC may never be involved in their consideration at all. The PAC does not generally deal with legislation. Legislation restricting or removing an Auditor-General's role is likely to be considered by another parliamentary committee without the depth of knowledge and commitment to the Auditor-General's role that a PAC would bring. PACs need to be vigilant to keep such proposals under review even if they are before another committee. PACs can press the case for greater public sector audit involvement in corporatised entities and in contracting-out relationships, and PACs must be vigilant to identify and support Auditors-General in resisting undesirable cuts in the Auditor-General's mandate.

In general, the Study Group believes that any company receiving public funding to deliver public services should be subject to the Auditor-General's audit mandate in respect of those services. This means that the Auditor-General should have access to the records of those companies by law. But also, in devising such outsourcing arrangements, it should be made clear to contractors that a measure of public sector accountability is one of the conditions under which they will be expected to operate. This can obviate misunderstandings arising later over the Auditor-General's role.

Commercial confidence

A further problem that increasingly arises from outsourcing arrangements is excessive claims to confidentiality on commercial grounds. The Study Group acknowledges commercial confidentiality as a legitimate factor for parliamentary committees to take into account in their information requests. But if such claims are acceded to too readily, this will result in a serious diminution of parliamentary accountability for what are still publicly-funded services. In Australia the PAC has recently recommended a shift in the onus of proof in respect of claims for confidentiality. It suggests that the onus of demonstrating a need for confidentiality be placed squarely on the chief executive officer of the entity making the claim. Only when the case can be clearly made should confidentiality be conceded. Furthermore, the Study Group observes that there are means of disclosing information to the Auditor-General or the PAC short of full public disclosure. It may be that disclosure can be confined to the Auditor-General alone, or disclosure made in camera to the PAC, or disclosure made with names or other details suppressed. A number of techniques might be employed that would reconcile the entity's need for confidentiality with the public's interest in ensuring that there is adequate scrutiny of how public resources are used.

REPORTING

The work of Auditors-General needs to be reported to Parliament and to the wider community. The Study Group considered a number of factors related to how the Auditor-General communicates the result of the audit work to stakeholders.

Preparation of reports

In the preparation of a report it is now regarded as critical that the factual content of a report be thoroughly reviewed first with the department or agency that is the subject of the report. In the United Kingdom in particular this can be an extensive process to ensure that – whatever their disagreements on conclusions – the Auditor-General and the department are agreed on the facts that underlie those conclusions. PACs must expect and demand that Auditors-General do review findings of fact with departments before making a report. Furthermore, natural justice requires that any adverse conclusions that the Auditor-General is minded to make about a department or an official are disclosed to the department or official first, and an opportunity is afforded for comment on the draft finding. No adverse finding can be included in a report unless the person concerned has first been given an adequate opportunity to change the Auditor-General's mind on it. If this has not happened there has inevitably been a failure of process.

The Study Group's main concern with the preparation of reports is to urge that they be drafted in a readable and interesting form. They must be made attractive and presentable.

Busy PAC members in particular must be able to digest the material easily. While they should not lose their value as informative documents they ought not to contain material that is too technical. Looking beyond PACs and Members of Parliament, Auditors-General's reports gain authority from being accepted by the wider public. Gaining this wider constituency's interest and support is a further reason for stressing the importance of presentation. Indeed Auditors-General as public figures need to give consideration to devising active communication strategies geared to the circumstances existing in their own countries and political systems. This can include close liaison with the news media, briefing members and departments before presentation of their reports, and use of websites. The latter is a particularly good medium to make information available to a wider public (but one must be careful to keep it up to date).

REPORTING TO PARLIAMENT

It is a fundamental principle that Auditors-General report to Parliament. This usually involves an unrestricted right of presenting reports to Parliament, though some countries, for example Canada, may restrict the number of special reports that an Auditor-General can present in any one year. In Canada too, special audits of Crown corporations are provided to the corporation's board and only exceptionally to Parliament. This is intended to reflect the arms-length relationship of such corporations with Parliament. But Parliaments do not just expect a single annual report. They expect Auditors-General to report on a continuous basis as circumstances dictate.

As part of a communications strategy, briefings for members immediately before tabling of a report are to be commended. This will enable members to utilise the contents of a report in the House as soon as it is made public. Briefings can be combined with a press lock-up that is designed to promote interest in and understanding of the issues discussed in the report.

Follow-up to reports

Most follow-up strategies involve the PAC. In effect, the Auditor-General enlists the good offices of the PAC. This usually means that Auditors-General's reports automatically stand referred to the PAC as they become available. In Australia the PAC has a statutory responsibility to review all tabled reports of the Auditor-General.

The PAC cannot follow up all Auditors-General reports, much less every issue raised in them. In India the PAC asks ministries to furnish notes on remedial or corrective action taken on audit recommendations. In Ontario the Provincial Auditor follows up all recommendations within two years to ascertain what action has occurred. In all cases it makes good sense for PACs and Auditors-General to co-ordinate their follow-up actions so that these are mutually reinforcing. The object is to ensure that departments review their practices in the light of Auditors-General recommendations, and explain what they have done to improve the matter that has given rise to concern.

Audit performance

Finally, it is important that Auditors-General themselves take steps to measure their own performance. Indicators for measuring audit performance that have been identified include actions taken on audit recommendations; savings achieved; and the frequency of references made to audit findings by legislators during their deliberations and representations in Parliament. Attention to such indicators is essential, for the effects of a successfully operating public audit system can be dramatic. As has already been mentioned, in Ontario it has been estimated that C$500 million of savings have resulted from audit recommendations over a period of eight years, plus an unquantifiable contribution to improving the administration and delivery of government services. Auditor-General accountability requires attention to such factors on the part of Auditors-General and parliamentary committees monitoring their performance.

Public Accounts Committees

THE ROLE OF THE PAC

The first PAC, and the prototype for the many other PACs that have been established throughout the Commonwealth since, was established by resolution of the House of Commons at Westminster in 1861 to be a permanent piece of Commons' financial machinery for exercising effective control over the appropriation of public moneys. While most countries do have a committee that is identifiable as a PAC (by whatever precise name it is called), some have absorbed the work of a PAC into that of a committee with a much wider remit. This is especially true of smaller jurisdictions. Whatever the precise arrangements in each country, the need for the Parliament to exercise oversight of the appropriations that it has authorised has led to the establishment of committees of members as a more efficient means of discharging this task than through the Parliament as a whole.

The PAC helps Parliament hold the government to account for its use of public funds and resources by examining the public accounts. Its terms of reference can be expressed narrowly by concentrating on financial probity and regularity, or its terms of reference can be expressed more widely by being conceived in performance audit terms, with the PAC being charged with examining the effectiveness of programmes in achieving their objectives. The PAC has an independent audit oversight on Parliament's behalf of the government and the public service.

Other committees

The PAC is not, however, likely to be the only parliamentary committee exercising an oversight function over the government that can extend into financial reporting. Increasingly, wider remits are being conceded to departmentally-based committees. This means that Auditors-General's reports are likely to be of interest to them and to fall within their remits too. Normally such departmentally-based committees are not subject to rules or conventions restraining them from the examination of policy, as PACs often are. As has already been discussed (pp. 30–1), such committees should be able to utilise the assistance of the Auditor-General too.

The remit of a PAC is as wide as the extent of the public sector, so it is no surprise that PACs have to find ways of managing the large number of demands on their time. Some of the techniques that may be employed (for example, subcommittees) are discussed later in this chapter, but one thing that PACs should consider before embarking upon a major inquiry is whether another parliamentary committee might be a better vehicle to pursue the matter. If policy issues are likely to figure prominently in the inquiry and these could therefore pose problems for a PAC, a departmentally-based committee that is free of such constraints would be able to handle the matter better. Also it may be preferable for a committee with a more specialist remit – defence, public lands, health and so on – to pursue a particular inquiry rather than a PAC, which is by definition multi-subject. (Though this is also an advantage, of course, giving the PAC an opportunity to take a whole-of-government approach, not limited to one sector.) So the PAC should also consider the contribution that other committees within the parliamentary system can make and, where appropriate, see it as its role to promote their utilisation.

Relationship with the Auditor-General

The relationship between the PAC and the Auditor-General has already been discussed from the point of view of the Auditor-General (see p. 31). An important part of a PAC's mandate is to help to ensure the independence of the Auditor-General and to bolster the effectiveness of that office. In this sense the PAC's role is derived from that of the Auditor-General rather than the PAC being an investigative body in its own right. In 1861 the legislative reforms that resulted in the creation of the office of Comptroller and Auditor-General were accompanied by procedural reforms that led to the establishment of the PAC. These reforms were seen as part of one package, and this has historically reinforced the interdependence of the two entities.

It is undoubtedly true that the work of the Auditor-General is, and ought to be, the staple of the PAC. Even in Canada where, as has been seen above, the PAC maintains an arms-length relationship with the Auditor-General during the conduct of its inquiries, at least 95 per cent of the committee's time is spent considering the Auditor-General's reports. In Australia the PAC is under a statutory obligation to review all reports from the Auditor-General that are tabled in Parliament. Most Commonwealth Parliaments confirm that the PAC's work depends primarily on the Auditor-General's reports. The Study Group considers that it is inevitable and desirable that the main focus of PAC work should be guided by the work of the Auditor-General. Close consultation on the Auditor-General's work programme should ensure a coincidence of interest in any event. Were the two bodies to be entirely uninterested in each other's programmes, public sector accountability would suffer greatly in its effectiveness.

Nevertheless, we do not see the PAC as merely a parliamentary mirror of the Auditor-General. The PAC should itself have the ability to pursue matters of concern to its members regardless of whether those matters are the subject of an Auditor-General's report. This is so even in those jurisdictions in which there is an especially close correspondence between the work of the Auditor-General and the work of the PAC.

Having acknowledged that, it is the case that any pursuit of a matter by the PAC will be more profitable if it is informed in the first place by an Auditor-General's report. While both the PAC and the Auditor-General are independent in their own spheres, they will function more effectively if they co-ordinate their work and operate in a mutually reinforcing fashion.

Aspects of a PAC's terms of reference

PACs examine the Public Accounts, the Auditor-General's Reports and matters relating to the effective and efficient use of money appropriated by Parliament. This can involve the PAC in spending much of its time examining departmental annual accounts. But other departmentally-based committees may do some of this work too.

The PAC is not generally concerned with macro-economic policy, though it may examine policies with major economic implications in the course of its work. Revenue collection and borrowing powers may come under review by PACs as part of their examination of the effectiveness of programmes. The administration of the processes of assessing and collecting tax, rather than the objectives of tax policy, are clearly matters which PACs may wish to examine. Similarly, while it may not be for a PAC to express an opinion on a government's decision to borrow funds, the management of a government's borrowing programme, and the decisions it makes to refinance loans at particular rates of interest or on particular terms, are matters on which a PAC may legitimately ask officials to answer to it. We have indicated above the limited role that an Auditor-General has in examining the government's budget (see p. 40). This applies to the PAC too. It will be the role of the Estimates Committee or a committee with a policy remit to examine the budget and to consider the budget's macro-economic assumptions. The budget involves matters of high policy and it is not appropriate for the PAC to be involved in its consideration. A similarly restrained role would be played by the PAC in relation to the central bank, mirroring the audit role performed by the Auditor-General.

Local authorities do not generally fall within a PAC's remit, as PACs tend to be concerned with central government accountability through Parliament. Local authorities are politically accountable to their local communities. In this case there may be a dichotomy between the PAC's mandate and that of the Auditor-General, since many Auditors-General have responsibility for auditing local authorities. At the other extreme, PACs may have an international role in respect of quasi-federal relationships into which their countries may enter. The United Kingdom's PAC is considering the extent to which it can investigate activities of the European Union to which the United Kingdom contributes substantial sums. The committee has already published reports on aspects of the work of the EU and on the operation of the United Kingdom arms of the EU.

Finally, a PAC, like any parliamentary committee, may have particular matters referred to it from time to time. It does not usually have legislation referred to it but it is conceivable that a major overhaul of public finance legislation, for example, could be referred to a PAC for its examination. In Canada since 1987 the Auditor-General's estimates have been referred to the PAC for examination. The Chair of the PAC has been consulted on the appointment of a new Auditor-General, and once a new Auditor-General has been appointed the committee may choose to interview the appointee. It is always competent for a legislature to make ad hoc referrals of subjects to a PAC for inquiry, though if this became too frequent it would interfere with the PAC's ability to carry out its regular work.

STATUS OF THE PAC

Ideally a PAC would be seen as Parliament's pre-eminent committee, with service on it considered to be a matter of prestige. It has been described as a miniature Parliament. But it must be acknowledged that it can be difficult to recruit Members to serve on such committees, even apart from the fact that only a small number of Members may be available.

Members' reluctance to serve on PACs can be a result of the fact that Members wish to use their committee service to engage with policy issues, as opposed to the PAC's focus on accountability. While there are Members who prefer to deal with accountability issues, the perception is that most Members today are more policy-oriented in their interests. Furthermore, Members with particular subject interests are likely to seek membership of the appropriate departmentally-based committee, rather than the PAC whose general remit is not likely to allow Members often to indulge in their preferred interests. PAC membership can be a good grounding in investigative work, which gives Members a broad knowledge of the machinery of government. This knowledge can then be used profitably by Members in their subsequent parliamentary work. But it is not the first love of many Members.

Another disadvantage of PAC work that is often felt by Members is that there are few political rewards from such work, especially where PACs adhere to strong conventions eschewing policy and striving for unanimity. In these circumstances membership of the PAC may not be a good political career path to choose. In a competitive environment such as that within Parliament, the advantage for one's reputation with party colleagues of membership of the PAC will not be readily apparent. This is especially the case for government Members who may feel inhibited in their PAC work and defensive about its outcomes. It is a better opportunity for opposition Members to do investigative work and bring information out, but they too must act with political restraint or risk the conventions of the PAC breaking down.

These factors can make membership of the PAC a career-inhibitor. Thus a problem that the Study Group has identified is how to make membership of the PAC career-enhancing. While acknowledging that the need for political reward is an essential element of any Member's career. and that Members generally are more interested in policy issues, we consider that some of the steps that we discuss in this report can elevate the PAC and membership of it into an aspect of parliamentary work that can attract a sufficient core of Members to ensure that it functions effectively. As a start, therefore, we do suggest that Parliaments regard the PAC as their pre-eminent committee and that any parliamentary steps that reinforce this impression be taken. As an example of such a step, we were told that in Australia the Public Accounts Committee and the Foreign Affairs Committee are jointly regarded as that Parliament's pre-eminent committees, and to reflect this the chairs of those committees are paid a salary higher than the salaries paid to the chairs of the other committees.

MEMBERSHIP OF THE PAC

The typical size of the PAC is eleven members, with it varying in size between large and small countries: the average in Asian Parliaments being 17 and that in Caribbean Parliaments being six (see Questionnaire). Even where the Chair is an opposition member, party membership of the PAC is usually proportionate to party membership in the House, with a government majority on the committee. This can result in a problem in finding Members to serve on the PAC, especially in Parliaments with smaller numbers of Members that do not have a sufficient pool of government backbench Members on which to draw. Nevertheless, it is important that all sides of the House participate in PAC work. It should not be seen as the sole preserve of opposition Members, for example, for if it were, it would be held in a different and less prestigious regard from a PAC that manages to bring together constructively Members from different parties.

We consider it critically important that efforts be made to associate senior opposition figures with the committee's work. An obvious way to do this is to follow the United Kingdom convention of an opposition Member chairing the committee. In that case it is always an opposition Member who was formerly a Treasury minister. But whether an opposition Member chairs the committee or not, we see a gain in prestige from the association of senior Members, opposition and government, with the work of the committee.

The PAC is made up of busy Members who may find it difficult to give their attention to the complex issues on which it is involved. But this is a common problem for other committees too. The Study Group does not favour special payment for service on the PAC as opposed to service on any other committee, as this might promote token service. Absences of members during public examinations of witnesses are a particular problem for PACs and are to be avoided if at all possible. PAC examination should be regarded by the civil service as the most onerous form of direct accounting to Parliament. Part of the prestige for PACs for which we strive derives from this perception. If PAC members absent themselves, witnesses will become sceptical about its seriousness of purpose and the PAC will begin to lose the Star Chamber aura which we see as attaching to it. It beholds PAC members themselves to act so as to maintain its prestige by not absenting themselves from its important public meetings. Reverting to a point already discussed, the fact that the political rewards of membership of the PAC are few, demands even greater self-motivation from its members in the way that they carry out their work.

Finally, there is the question of turnover in membership. Most Parliaments appoint their membership for the term of the Parliament, though some serve for shorter periods than this. A rapid turnover in the membership of any body is undesirable. Effectiveness is promoted by continuity of membership during a Parliament and also by an admixture of members with experience of the PAC working together with new members who bring fresh experiences and their own enthusiasms to the task. In general, longevity of membership will strengthen the PAC. The Study Group recommends that Parliaments seek to ensure that there is always sufficient experience and seniority among the membership of the PAC.

TRAINING

Members who are assigned to serve on PACs cannot be assumed to have any in-depth knowledge of accountability issues as they relate to government, nor any understanding of the role of the PAC in reinforcing accountability. Indeed, given the general policy preoccupations of Members, it is unlikely that even an experienced Member who is appointed to the PAC for the first time will be well equipped to understand the new issues that he or she will confront. Part of the process of building capacity within Parliaments needs to be devoted to increasing the ability of Members of Parliament to comprehend accountability issues.

This capacity building can start at the outset of a Member's career. Many Parliaments are now organising orientation or induction training courses for their new Members and for existing Members who wish to participate in them. It is not possible or profitable to deal with the PAC in depth at such a time, but Members should be made aware of it and of the special role it has to play. Maximum effort has to be put into fulfilling Members' training needs when they are first appointed to the PAC. It is essential to attempt to define more precisely what these training needs might be. The Study Group understands that Monash University in Melbourne is carrying out some research in this area, and we will be very interested in its results. Some of the things that we would see the training cover include reading and understanding the Public Accounts documents and familiarity with the structure of government at the departmental/agency level. Any training would also need to introduce Members to the work of the Auditor-General and should invite Members to reflect on their roles as members of the PAC, stimulating them to ask what they are expected or could be expected to achieve in those roles.

One 'in-house' source for some of this training that was suggested is retired Chairs of PACs and Auditors-General from that or other countries. Their experiences and insights would be most valuable to Members in a very practical sense, and we encourage those organising training for PACs to consider using them as possible contributors. Universities are another source for training, either as part of courses they already offer or by specially-devised sessions commissioned for the PAC. Indeed, universities could build into such sessions presentations and interaction with former Chairs of PACs and Auditors-General.

Looking further afield, international agencies too can contribute to capacity building in assisting with PAC training needs on a global or regional basis, by organising workshops or expert visits. The CPA has an ongoing project funding study tours by presiding officers to other CPA branches. This project has recently been enhanced by the Executive Committee to include Parliamentarians who have particular roles, such as chairing a committee. This latest extension has the potential to assist in capacity building in respect of PAC work. The Commonwealth Secretariat is developing in-house skills programmes to build capacity within committee systems generally by supporting suitable resource persons to visit Parliaments to help with training. These programmes can be accessed through the CPA or through conventional diplomatic channels. In some cases training may take the form of distance learning modules for individual Members to work through at their own pace. The Internet now provides a swift means of communication which enhances the effectiveness of such training tools. The use of the Internet to disseminate information on PAC practice can also contribute to satisfying Members' training needs: for example news groups on PAC matters could be organised from time to time and the existence of a website containing a compendium of PAC practice would provide Members with an information resource on which they could draw. (These matters are discussed further on pp. 90–2.)

The training needs of staff serving PACs must be recognised too. There is no reason why staff cannot participate in many of the training initiatives and benefit from the information sources that we have discussed above. Generally, staff will change less rapidly than PAC membership, and even staff who have never served with the PAC before are likely to have had some governmental experience, thus making them familiar with the government structure. Nevertheless they need to be kept up to date by exposure to the materials and training we have discussed. A further means of staff training is by arranging secondments and exchanges with other Parliaments' PACs so that a cross-fertilisation of ideas and experiences is promoted. The CPA programme already mentioned provides opportunities for parliamentary staff to visit other branches too. The opportunity to arrange secondments, exchanges or visits within the Commonwealth, bilaterally or with international agency support, is always there, and should be given serious consideration.

THE CHAIR OF THE PAC

Manner of appointment

There are a number of different ways within the Commonwealth by which the Chair of the PAC is chosen. In some countries, for example, India and Botswana, the Speaker appoints the Chair. In others, a selection committee makes the choice. In most countries the PAC elects its own Chair – occasionally by secret ballot, otherwise following the normal procedures for the election of committee chairs generally. These great differences in the technique of choosing a Chair are not necessarily significant in themselves. They are likely to have evolved out of the conventions or expectations associated with the role of Chair of the PAC in that particular country, and the similarities between Parliaments in regard to these are greater than the mechanics of the appointment process might suggest. For example, India and the United Kingdom have very different processes for appointing the Chair of the PAC. In the case of the former the Speaker makes the appointment, while in the case of the latter the PAC (which has a government majority) elects the Chair. However, in both countries by convention (in India since 1967) an opposition member is chosen as Chair and that Chair chairs the committee in a consensual manner. Despite the different processes followed in electing a Chair, a similar outcome in both countries is expected to result from that choice. The Study Group does not regard the different methods of appointing a Chair as being of great significance.

Government/opposition chairs

In two-thirds of cases PACs are chaired by an opposition member (see Questionnaire). In some countries, such as India and the United Kingdom, this is a very strong convention. In many countries the PAC is the sole exception to the practice of government Members chairing committees, which is a clear demonstration of the fact that the PAC's unique role is appreciated. However, although the majority of Commonwealth Parliaments do provide opposition chairs for the PAC there are equally respectable arguments against this. In Australia it is considered advantageous to have a government Member as Chair, as this can assist with the implementation of the PAC's recommendations. It is regarded as the duty of the Chair to advocate that the PAC's recommendations be taken up and implemented by the government. This can involve behind the scenes work persuading reluctant ministers to act. A government Member can do this more effectively than an opposition Member who as a political opponent will not have the confidence of ministers. In Australia generally, at the federal and state levels, government Members are seen as more effective Chairs of PACs for this reason.

The Study Group considered that what is of first importance is the capacity of the Chair to carry out the duties of the office effectively, rather than whether he or she is drawn from the government or the opposition ranks.

Role

The Chair is extremely important in ensuring the effective operation of the PAC. As well as the formal powers of the position, the Chair of the PAC plays a principal role as the representative of the PAC to the House and to the wider public. This role goes much further than discharging the duties of presiding over the committee. The Chair is a public figure by virtue of the fact that he or she is chairing the PAC and will be expected to comment on matters from that perspective. Such comments must therefore be couched in terms that conform to the conventions and working practices of the PAC. The Chair, even when commenting outside the committee, cannot play an overly partisan role in that capacity. The Chair may be an ex officio member of bodies outside Parliament, and can expect to be consulted about or to play a role in, the appointment of the Auditor-General. Furthermore, the Chair will be expected to advance the interests of the PAC outside its meetings by pressing ministers to implement its recommendations and seeking full co-operation with its work from the bureaucracy.

The Chair of the PAC, whether a government or an opposition Member, must act more independently of party pressures than the chairs of other committees. One major reason for this (discussed at page 71) is the practice (consistent among PACs) of striving for consensus or unanimity. A chair of a committee that functions solely on the basis of the government's in-built majority does not need to reach out to opposition members (though such a chair may in fact do so, so as to facilitate the smooth working of the committee). That is not the way that a PAC should function. Consequently the Chair of the PAC must be continually working to maintain harmony within the total membership of the committee. What is important is not which party the Chair is drawn from, but whether the Chair has the personal qualities needed to achieve this objective.

In sum, the choice of Chair of the PAC should not be capricious. It will clearly be of advantage if the person appointed Chair has had previous PAC experience, but this cannot always be guaranteed. The person concerned needs to be of sufficient standing and authority as a parliamentarian to maintain the committee's prestige and co-operative working practices. The Chair must regard himself or herself as the representative of the entire committee and seek to advance its interests in better parliamentary accountability. Linked with this is the desirability of not changing the Chair too often. The Chair needs a reasonable length of time to establish his or her position and to lead the committee effectively. Ideally the Chair should remain in office throughout the term of the Parliament.

RESOURCES

As is to be expected, the resources provided to PACs vary considerably between countries. In India the PAC has 22 staff and its own libraries equipped with literature and reports. On the other hand small or developing countries' PACs may not have staff dedicated to them at all, and have to share whatever staffing and resources that the Parliament possesses with other committees. Staff of the Auditor-General's office can assist the PAC and to some extent can be used to compensate for the lack of the PAC's own resources. But, of course, whether this is possible depends in turn upon the Auditor-General's resources. A lack of resource for the Auditor-General can in this way impair the effectiveness of the PAC, first by impacting on the Auditor-General's ability to report to Parliament and secondly by limiting the staff assistance that the Auditor-General can give to the PAC. Other possible sources of assistance for the PAC are departmental staff, especially from the Treasury, who may have expertise that can assist the committee. But such staff may also have an official interest in the committee's inquiries and consequently it may not be appropriate to use them. Finally, the universities may be able to provide assistance in particular areas.

If PAC capacity is to be enhanced, sufficient resources in terms of staff and equipment, particularly computer facilities, need to be made available to it. Adequate funding is a perennial problem. But the international imperatives for an effective PAC that we have discussed above suggest that the international community too has an interest in ensuring that PACs are adequately resourced to do the job that is expected of them. It is not sufficient merely to establish a PAC if it cannot then function properly due to lack of resources. Priority needs to be given to adequately resourcing the operations of PACs. How this is achieved depends upon each Parliament's arrangements for determining its own funding and what international contributions may be available.

EXAMINATION OF POLICY

The extent to which a PAC can examine and make judgements on matters of policy is an extremely important issue. From it there flows a number of consequences in terms of practices that a committee follows in going about its work. A PAC which makes policy judgements will find it difficult to maintain unanimity conventions among its membership in respect of those judgements. Such judgements are, by definition, likely to be contentious and to bring the committee into conflict with the government at a ministerial – not just a departmental – level. In these circumstances it will be very difficult for a PAC to achieve unanimity or consensus. Furthermore, if policy judgements are to be made, the range of witnesses and advice that the PAC will need to obtain is likely to be greater. It would not be possible, for instance, to hear only from officials if the committee makes a practice of examining the merits of policy.

In general, those PACs that eschew policy judgements have higher expectations of achieving consensus on their reports and tend to confine themselves to hearing from departmental witnesses.

In fact, most PACs do not question the underlying policy behind a programme. This is regarded as something for ministers to answer for on the floor of the House. PACs concentrate on how policy is implemented, rather than on the policy itself. But, it must be admitted, this is not always an easy distinction to make. It is difficult to frame an acceptable definition of the 'policy' being implemented in any particular case, for this can depend upon the level of generality at which the policy is described. For instance, governments may themselves regard the method of implementation of a programme to be part of their policy, for example, whether its delivery is to be in public or private hands. The ownership of the delivery agent can in one sense be looked upon as an administrative matter within the purview of the PAC. However, the ownership issue may be critically important to a government as expressing its own political philosophy. In this sense, which mode of delivery is chosen is itself a highly significant policy decision. Would a PAC be justified in criticising the ownership model in these circumstances?

The issues for parliamentary scrutiny arising from outsourcing have been discussed above (pp. 47–50); this question is posed only to illustrate the fact that it is not always easy to follow a policy/administration split. Perhaps one way of doing so is to be guided by one of the consequences of not examining policy: the fact that where policy is not examined departmental officials are the witnesses who appear before the PAC, not ministers. This keeps the focus on administration and away from policy. If the PAC concentrates on issues that departmental officials can be expected to respond to, rather than on issues that ministers would be expected to respond to, it will, in this rather oblique way, avoid trespassing into matters of policy. In practice, rather than having PACs settle on a comprehensive definition of what is policy and then apply that definition to particular circumstances, it is best to work pragmatically through issues with officials, judging whether it is appropriate to deal with a matter by the appropriateness of the committee's interaction with those officials.

In some countries PACs are not under policy constraints. In these cases, minority reports are more likely to occur and the committees are more likely to need to hear from ministers as part of their work. This can in itself provoke confrontation. However, even where a PAC does not examine policy questions, it may see fit to criticise a policy that is leading to obvious waste or not producing the desired results. It is not a PAC's job to suggest alternative policies, but in clear cases of policy failure a PAC may draw attention to it as a matter of public audit.

Unanimity

Some PACs have an invariable rule that recommendations must be concurred in by all members of the committee. This is the case in India, for example, and it adds immeasurably to the strength of a committee's recommendations that they are known to emanate from all members of the PAC, irrespective of party. Australia and the United Kingdom also have very strong conventions of PACs striving for unanimity in their conclusions, with very few instances of divisions or dissents being recorded. There is no doubt that it can be more difficult to reach conclusions where such a strong convention exists, but the process of working for agreement in such circumstances can help to foster a sense of teamwork since each member's view is of critical and equal importance if unanimity is to be achieved. On the other hand, other PACs regularly record minority views in their reports, with decisions being taken on the basis of votes that follow party lines.

In general, a principle of absolute unanimity in PAC decisions is regarded as too exacting a standard and is not insisted upon by most Parliaments. But it seems to the Study Group that while unanimity on all occasions may be unrealistic, it is necessary for PACs to strive for some consensus over their reports. If this is achieved their reports will carry much more weight than if they are merely seen as party documents. The Chair's role is important here, as has already been remarked, in trying to bring members of the committee together to work harmoniously during their inquiries and into some general agreement at their conclusion.

WORKING PRACTICES

Frequency of meetings

There are huge variations throughout the Commonwealth in the frequency with which PACs meet. In some countries the PAC may meet only once or twice a year and in some cases not at all. On the other hand, the PAC may meet as often as twice a week while Parliament is in session. These differences often reflect the different meeting patterns of Parliaments themselves, which range from short, infrequent meetings during the year to almost continuous sittings.

Committees that meet on a frequent basis have a better opportunity of promoting consensual working practices than committees whose members come together infrequently. While endorsing the desirability of regular PAC meetings, the Study Group recognises that the practicability of this depends upon each Parliament's own circumstances.

Meeting in public or in private

The work carried out by PACs can be highly technical. Partly for this reason and also because policy has not generally been the concern of PACs and they have endeavoured to work consensually, it has been the case that PACs have usually worked away from the glare of publicity. Indeed, the lack of political or public recognition for members who serve on the PAC has been identified as a drawback to attracting members to it as a career path (see page 61). To some extent these factors have been seen as going with the territory. A low key approach to publicity on the part of the PAC has helped to discourage members from grandstanding and thus endangering the consensual manner in which such committees generally approach their work. There is a strong view that the PAC works best away from the attentions of the media. The Study Group would not wish to encourage any developments which inhibited PACs working together in the effective manner that many of them have developed.

On the other hand, there does seem to be an increasing desire for PACs to sit in public to hear evidence from the departments under scrutiny. It seems to be inevitable that PACs too should expose their proceedings to public view, as demands for greater openness generally are made. Apart from this reactive approach, public sessions have been seen in a positive light in helping to raise the profile of scrutiny work and to build a public constituency for the work carried out by the PAC. Some Parliaments report significant improvements in the responses from ministers and departments when the PAC started sitting in public for the receipt of evidence. This allowed more media attention to be paid to the PAC than had been the case. Those committees that have opened their proceedings to the public have not reported any deleterious long-term effects such as greater reticence on the part of witnesses or a breaking-down of conventions among members.

It does seem that, apart from the hearing of evidence which has a security or commercial confidentiality implication, a greater public knowledge of the committee's proceedings is desirable. It is incumbent on the PAC to promote greater public awareness of its role in the internationally important task of scrutinising public sector performance. The PAC's work is performed through Parliament for the public benefit; it is therefore fitting that the public should know as much about it as possible without interfering with its effective performance. Hearing evidence in public is one way of ensuring that this is the case.

Subcommittees

The great enemy of effective scrutiny through PACs is the difficulty for members to find the time to perform the work that it demands. One way, if their constituent rules allow, is to form subcommittees to perform particular tasks. Not all PACs do this by any means, many regarding it as essential that the full PAC share in the judgements that are made on departments and officials. However, even with those PACs that employ subcommittees to undertake detailed inquiries, the endorsement and adoption of their conclusions by the full PAC is essential, and it is the PAC that makes a report to Parliament, not the subcommittee.

Subcommittees can be used as standing committees to consider particular subject areas (defence, health, and so on) that are otherwise undifferentiated in the amorphous remit of a PAC. In this way a subcommittee can be used as a means of indulging a Member's particular subject interest, and attracting to the PAC a Member who might otherwise prefer to serve on a subject committee (see p. 62). Other subcommittee arrangements might see particular inquiries carried out by ad hoc subcommittees which cease to exist as such once they have reported to the main committee. Finally, subcommittees may be used to give a support service to the main committee, as in Canada where all committees, including the PAC, form an agenda subcommittee to draw up a detailed work programme for the main committee to adopt.

The Study Group therefore sees subcommittees as a useful organisational tool for PACs to consider using.

Witnesses

As has been mentioned above, committees that do not examine policy issues generally confine themselves to hearing evidence from departmental officials to emphasise their non-policy orientations. Even committees that do examine policy rely in the main on departmental witnesses. It is overwhelmingly true that the work of the PAC involves interaction with officials. As well as departmental witnesses, the Auditor-General is also commonly heard as a witness before PACs, quite apart from the adviser function that that officer performs (see p. 32). Ministers are seldom witnesses to PACs, and in any case only when PACs have a policy remit expressly conferred on them or where no convention of avoiding policy judgements exists. PACs can hear evidence outside these categories from statutory authorities, interest groups and other individuals, though this is much less common than from departmental officials.

PACs generally do not regard themselves as grievance committees taking complaints from individuals who allege that they have been the subject of improper or unfair treatment. Such complaints, if received directly by the PAC, are likely to be referred to the Ombudsman, a minister, another committee or a department rather than followed up directly by the PAC. PACs regard themselves as responsible for considering systemic issues as opposed to individual complaints. For these latter matters, other parliamentary channels exist.

REPORTING

In some cases the PAC issues only one report each year or once each session to the Parliament on all work on which it has been engaged during the course of that time. But generally PACs report to the legislature as they see fit, and their reports can deal with a number of issues or can relate to a single investigation which the PAC considers warrants communication to the House in a stand-alone report.

It may be that the PAC decides that a particular matter does not require to be dealt with in a report to the House. For example, the publicity attendant on a hearing may be considered to have satisfactorily resolved the issues that led to the inquiry being launched in the first place. The transcript of the hearings and any press reports of it may form a sufficient record of the issue and thus obviate a report. However, this must be regarded as exceptional. Even where the hearings do satisfactorily resolve the concerns that led to the inquiry in the first place, a confirmatory note to that effect in the PAC's annual or general report would be appropriate. Even in the United Kingdom, where the system of extensive consultation between the Auditor-General and the department concerned means that the vast majority of cases brought to the PAC have been satisfactorily resolved beforehand, the PAC will issue reports on the matters that it has inquired into.

Increasingly Parliaments are posting all select committee reports on a parliamentary website, and this means that PAC reports are now much more widely available than before. As well as select committee reports, parliamentary websites contain the minutes of proceedings and the transcript of evidence where one has been made. PACs may issue press releases to draw attention to a report that they have presented, and if the matter is important enough may also hold a press conference. A further means of disseminating PAC reports is to ask Auditors-General to include a section in their reports listing or summarising PAC reports and to include or link PAC reports to any Auditor-General's website. The Study Group endorses the use of the Internet to disseminate information on the work of PACs, and also welcomes further publicity steps being taken to raise public awareness of all of the more important reports which they present.

Findings

A critical PAC report can have important repercussions. It can lead to important changes in public sector organisation and systems. Indeed many if not most of these will have been identified by the Auditor-General in the prior investigation carried out by that officer. Much of the PAC's work is designed to function as part of the follow-up process to the Auditor-General's inquiries (see p. 56). But PAC reports may also result from inquiries that were not initiated first by the Auditor-General, and these may lead to recommendations for organisational and systems changes.

An important factor for PACs to consider is the effect their reports may have on the careers of individual public servants. This raises the question of how far the PAC may go in fixing responsibility on individuals for faults that it finds. In cases where the PAC believes that there has been fraud or corruption the matter should be handed over to the proper authorities (police, serious fraud office, and so on) for inquiry. Certainly PACs should not attempt to make findings on criminal culpability. That is a matter for the courts, and any PAC finding on the matter could only prejudice a successful prosecution.

The PAC may however feel that the conduct of individuals, while not criminal, has fallen seriously below the standards expected of a public servant. Is it appropriate to name and criticise an individual in such a circumstance? There is a conflict of view on this point.

On one view the bureaucracy can too easily escape responsibility by avoiding any assumption of individual responsibility. The civil service is too ready to defend its own behind a wall of anonymity. Responsibility is effectively avoided in such circumstances. Thus some authority external to the departmental structure with disciplinary powers over officials is justified. In France, the equivalent of the PAC is said to have power to fine delinquent officials. This is a power that could be considered for PACs generally.

Against this is the view that it is not the PAC's role to impose penalties or even to fix individual responsibilities. Governments are responsible for imposing sanctions on their employees and for managing their resources efficiently. To allow the PAC to impose penalties on individuals raises questions of natural justice which would necessitate it following elaborate procedures before reaching such conclusions. It would also tend to make public servants highly risk averse in their approaches so as to avoid such censure.

These opposing views each have much to commend them. To some extent, the role that the PAC performs in this regard will depend upon what other effective mechanisms exist for disciplining civil servants and weeding out inefficiencies in the public sector. Where these mechanisms exist, the PAC can leave it to them to operate at the level of individual discipline. Where they do not exist the PAC may need to involve itself more at that level. Certainly PACs do not have the resources that are available to the departments that they inquire into. This does justify PACs placing the burden of proof on departments to demonstrate that they have carried out their duties effectively and efficiently. While we would not like to see a climate of suspicion existing between the PAC and the bureaucracy, officials must feel that in a very real sense they are obliged to justify their actions to the PAC, rather than the PAC having to uncover matters adverse to them. But the precise relationship between a PAC and the bureaucracy depends upon local circumstances.

Recommendations in PAC reports

Recommendations in a PAC report are made overwhelmingly to the government. This is right. It is the government that is responsible for managing the use of resources in the public sector and so it is the government that is obliged to deal with problems revealed by a PAC inquiry. Occasionally PAC reports may recommend that the Auditor-General follow up a particular matter, though this is unusual since the close relationship between the PAC and the Auditor-General enables such matters to be resolved in settling the Auditor-General's work programme.

The emphasis in PAC reports is inevitably on past performance, so much so that many of the problems dealt with in the reports may already have been resolved. This time lag between the event which has given rise to concern and the PAC's ability to address it in a report is a problem, and has led to a questioning of the relevance of some PAC work. Consequently some PACs, assisted by the Auditor-General, are attempting to initiate concurrent scrutiny, whereby a programme is examined as it is being implemented and any recommendations are made contemporaneously with its operation. This approach has the potential to bring a PAC's work more up to date. However, even with retrospective reporting PACs can use lessons learned to make recommendations that improve the delivery of programmes in the future by ensuring better financial and management controls and better flows of information.

FOLLOW-UP TO REPORTS

Responses

Ascertaining what action has been taken in response to the recommendations of the PAC is a critical aspect of measuring the PAC's effectiveness. The follow-up steps to a PAC report are therefore extremely important.

Most Parliaments require the government to respond formally to recommendations contained in a PAC report within a certain period of time. In some cases this may require extensive co-ordination of a government response where several departments or agencies are involved. Acceptance rates for PAC recommendations can be very high. The United Kingdom PAC has achieved an acceptance rate of 90 per cent. In India over the last six Parliaments the comparable figure is a 61 per cent acceptance rate. These governmental responses should be presented to Parliament for the information of members and the public.

Implementation

It is one thing to receive positive responses from the government, but PACs also need to know whether the government in fact implements the measures it has promised in its response. In many countries the Auditor-General plays a monitoring role, not only for recommendations in that officer's own reports but also for PAC recommendations. In Canada, for instance, the Auditor-General has a policy of following up two years later PAC recommendations and the introduction of changes announced by the government in response to them, in order to review their implementation. Auditors-General often make a practice of reporting back to PACs on whether and how their recommendations have been implemented. In regard to implementation, the United Kingdom Auditor-General's practice of agreeing facts with departments before a matter is brought to the PAC, while it can cause frustrating delays, is seen as an especially effective means of getting departmental 'buy-in' for implementation of PAC recommendation. Indeed these are effectively implemented as part of the process of inquiry rather than as an outcome of the findings.

Implementation can take the form of changes to or even the discontinuance of particular programmes, but even more valuable are the general lessons learned from a particular issue. These can lead to policy or procedural changes of general application across the public sector, for example on tendering processes to follow or standard provisions to include in certain types of contract.

Where a PAC is not satisfied with a response it can, of course, pursue the matter again with a further inquiry if it feels that this will be profitable. In Botswana, where the PAC is not satisfied with a response it has the option of referring the matter to the Ombudsman Commission or the Public Prosecutor for follow-up action. It is at this time that the qualities of the Chair and his or her ability to persuade the government to address PAC reports seriously are important. As has been pointed out (see page 66), it is sometimes seen as easier for a Chair from within the government ranks to work behind the scenes to ensure that Ministers take sufficient note of PAC recommendations and that any departmental pressure to ignore or reject them is resisted.

Debate

A debate in the House on PAC reports and government responses to them is not necessarily held in all Parliaments. Of course, PAC reports are on the public record and they can be used in parliamentary proceedings, for example, to form the basis of questions. But many Parliaments do not specifically debate them. The Indian legislatures, for example, do not normally debate PAC reports, and in Canada it is rare for such a debate to be held. In the United Kingdom an annual debate is held on up to six PAC reports.

This lack of response reflects the perennial problem of finding time on the floor of the House to debate every matter that might be considered worthy of attention. It is true that there is not time for everything, and governments will always seek to give parliamentary priority to their own legislative programmes. But PAC work is an essential part of the accountability demanded of governments as part of the price for being in government. It is not unreasonable to demand some parliamentary time for debate on PAC reports. The Study Group considers that the work of the PAC is of such critical importance in maintaining the integrity of a country's public sector that an annual debate on its work would appear essential. This would be a minimum acknowledgment from the Parliament that it takes seriously the need to ensure that the country's public sector is functioning properly and in the wider public interest. It is part of the accountability price that governments must pay in exchange for office.

Problems for developing countries and smaller Parliaments

The Study Group spent some time identifying the special problems faced by PACs in developing countries and smaller Parliaments. These two categories – developing countries and smaller Parliaments – do not necessarily overlap, although in practice they are likely to do so. We do not have a precise definition in mind of what a smaller Parliament is in terms of numbers, although probably around 60 Members or fewer is the category to which this description applies. With fewer than 60 members there are inherent problems for a PAC because there may be a lack of government Members to serve on the committee (and on parliamentary committees generally) given the large proportion of the Members who will hold ministerial office. The national Parliaments of most developed countries are larger than this (though not necessarily those of states or provinces within federations). For a number of developing countries with Parliaments of more than 60 Members the problems they face are not due to a lack of Members but rather of creating the capacity for PACs to carry out their work effectively.

RESOURCES

For PACs in developing countries resources are the crucial constraint on effective performance.

One of the most important means of improving PAC performance internationally that was identified by the Study Group is taking full advantage of information technology and, in particular, the Internet. There are obviously huge variances in the availability of IT and the Internet throughout the world. Until these access problems are addressed this will be a major constraint on building PAC capacity. However, there is a natural exponential growth in such access and this in itself is dramatically reducing the costs involved. Putting in place an IT infrastructure that permits economic development is a much wider question than how IT affects PAC capacity building, but the signs for IT and Internet growth in developing countries are encouraging.

PACs need strong support from the Auditor-General and committee staff. Thus, if the Auditor-General is not adequately resourced this will have serious implications for the PAC. The PAC relies largely on the information provided by the Auditor-General to guide and assist it in its work. Obviously if this is lacking it will impede the PAC in carrying out its work. A weak or ineffective Auditor-General will inevitably result in a weak or ineffective PAC. A major problem in obtaining adequate resources can be that the executive exercises excessive control over funding. The executive is not likely (mistakenly, we would maintain) to give priority to funding a parliamentary body that is exercising oversight of its activities. This is not a problem confined to developing countries or smaller Parliaments.

A rational local method of allocating parliamentary funding, one which takes account of the essential functions performed by oversight committees such as the PAC, is clearly needed. This is a matter for Parliament as a whole to attend to, it is not something that the PAC can deal with on its own. In addition, external agencies (such as, for example, the World Bank) can provide assistance and training for those Parliaments that need it. However, for any direct funding to be effective in enhancing the capacity of the PAC it must be tailored to the specific use of the PAC. Giving funding to Members of Parliament for unspecified uses would not guarantee that the funding would be used to build the capacity of the

PAC to carry out its work – for example, by boosting the size and expertise of its secretariat. It might be devoted to other unrelated parliamentary activities. Funding provided to help build PAC capacity needs to be specifically identified for use in ways that will directly contribute to such an end.

ATTENDANCE OF MEMBERS

A particular problem for smaller Parliaments that has been identified is the difficulty of finding Members to serve on the PAC and of getting Members to attend meetings. This problem is exacerbated where Members are on a number of committees. For smaller Parliaments too, meetings of committees, including that of the PAC, can only take place when Parliament is not sitting, since Members must necessarily give their attention to the Chamber. This can add to the cost of running Parliaments, since Members must remain in the capital during adjournments or return to it for meetings. Smaller Parliaments may have an especial difficulty in finding government Members to serve on the PAC, since ministerial office depletes the pool of government backbench Members available to serve.

In the case of smaller bicameral Parliaments, it makes sense for the two chambers to pool their memberships and form a joint PAC to ensure that the best use is made of the limited number of parliamentarians. But, of course, many smaller Parliaments are not bicameral. Another approach would be to co-opt non-Members of Parliament on to the PAC as non-voting members, to expand the PAC's range of membership skills. For smaller Parliaments, supplementing their membership in a way that does not alter the political outcome of the election is an option to compensate for the lack of personnel resources, especially to improve the effectiveness of Parliament's committee system.

This raises the question of remuneration for members of the PAC. Obviously, if non-Members were co-opted on to the PAC, a means of compensating them for their time or expenses incurred would need to be found. It was also suggested that, as a way of encouraging regular Members to take their membership of the PAC more seriously and to combat absenteeism, an enhanced salary should be paid to members of the PAC. It is already the case in some Parliaments, that the Chair of the PAC receives a greater salary than chairs generally.

The Study Group sees the question of an enhanced salary for the Chair as being different from that of a special salary for members of the PAC. We have already indicated that building up the position of the Chair is an important means of increasing the prestige of the PAC. An enhanced salary is one means of doing this. But that does not mean that we favour a special salary for all PAC members over and above members of other committees. To do that could create undesirable incentives for Members who might seek PAC membership for the wrong reasons. The fear was expressed that payment for service could result in token service. Members of other committees are likely to find it inequitable. The Study Group therefore favours specific attendance allowances, rather than increased salaries, as a means of overcoming attendance problems at PAC meetings by Members.

Where Auditors-General are adequately resourced, PACs should draw on the Auditor-General's office for secretariat assistance either on an 'as needed' basis or through a programme of regular secondments. Secondments of experts from overseas or from the secretariat of another Parliament are also, subject to funding being available, another way of providing capacity and helping to build capacity in the future, by local staff learning from the skills that the secondees have to impart. The use of the Internet to disseminate information about PACs for other Parliaments to use can help to close the information gap that might hamper PAC capacity development (see pp. 90–1). The Study Group also considered it necessary for Members to visit other Parliaments and learn directly from their counterparts how they discharge their functions and what experiences they have to impart. The CPA's study tours project can assist in this regard.

LACK OF LEGAL PROTECTIONS

Given the heavy reliance laid in developing countries on the Auditor-General's inspection functions as a means of counteracting corruption and fraud, it is particularly important for the Auditor-General and that officer's staff to have adequate legal protections to enable them to carry out their functions (see pp. 45–7).

LACK OF UNDERSTANDING OF PAC'S ROLE

Some of the difficulties faced by PACs in developing countries are not peculiar to those countries. Partisanship and playing to the gallery by members, misunderstanding and suspicion by the bureaucracy of the PAC's role, poor preparation by witnesses, lack of government responses, failure to implement PAC recommendations, and follow-up inquiries by the PAC being seen as a waste of time, were some of the problems experienced by PACs in developing countries that were identified by the Study Group. These are problems that can plague PACs in larger Parliaments in developed countries too. However, they are seen as being particularly acute in developing countries where PACs are not yet firmly established in their roles. Here we come back to the importance of the international element in the work of the PAC (see pp. 15–18). The PAC must be seen as an essential part of the attestation of the integrity and efficiency of a country's political and financial infrastructure.

Information exchanges

Perhaps the most effective way in which PAC performance in every country can be improved is by building up effective means of exchanging information. Information is a key resource in building capacity for the PAC to function well in the first place. It is just as essential for a well-established PAC to keep abreast of developments, identify trends and try to anticipate the constantly changing range of public audit issues with which it will sooner or later be confronted.

In this area, taking maximum advantage of information technology is crucial. The Internet now provides virtually instantaneous means of communication, and makes it possible to exchange information throughout the entire world on a scale and at a speed not contemplated a few years ago. There are always problems of information overload, of course, but, properly used, such tools make huge improvements in PAC performance realisable. Until access to these new technologies is improved for the developing nations, they will be under severe constraints in building capacity for their PACs.

ROLE OF THE CPA

The Study Group discussed the role that the CPA could play in promoting information interchange on PAC matters among its membership.

Any consideration of the CPA's role has to start from the position that the CPA is an organisation that essentially functions through its branches. Its permanent secretariat is very small in absolute terms (14 permanent staff) and is even smaller when this is considered in relative terms to the CPA's total membership (over 16,000 Members of Parliament). Any permanent administrative role could therefore only be accepted if an individual branch was willing to assume responsibility for performing it. A model for this is the Commonwealth Speakers and Presiding Officers Conference (a non-CPA organisation) in respect of which the Canadian House of Commons provides an ongoing secretariat. In a CPA context, the Commonwealth of Australia Branch maintains a regional secretariat for both the Australian and Pacific regions.

Subject to a branch being willing to accept a permanent servicing role of this nature, the CPA's role in promoting ongoing interchange on PAC matters is likely to be more of a catalyst to developments rather than as an administrator of a permanent programme. It is in this light that the discussion of the various options identified in this section proceeds.

INDIVIDUAL WEBSITES

Many Parliaments have now established their own websites containing information about their Parliament and its activities. The PAC may be part of this website or may have its own website linked to it. Websites containing information about every PAC (in particular its reports) are an obvious goal. Links between PAC websites could also be developed. Only by establishing such websites will information about the activities of the various PACs be disseminated to other PACs around the world.

A constant difficulty with websites is maintaining them and keeping them up to date. It is comparatively easy to start a website but it can become a burden to maintain. Failure to update information on websites is a serious problem as they can thereby become very misleading. Those Parliaments or PACs with sufficient staff resources should be able to cope with this issue, but many Parliaments will find it difficult to maintain their websites in an up to date condition.

One solution that was suggested was investigating whether the country's Auditor-General's office could maintain or help to maintain the PAC website. Auditors-General are themselves likely to have their own websites. We would not see it as appropriate for a PAC website to lose its identity by being subsumed into an Auditor-General's website, but effective collaboration between the two may help to overcome a lack of PAC resource. Another possibility is to use interns who wish to spend time in the Parliament as part of a university or training course to perform such tasks. This would be mutually beneficial for the Parliament in disseminating information and for the interns in helping them to gain a detailed knowledge of a particular aspect of parliamentary work. But such a solution would be dependent on the ability of persons who will of necessity be on short-term attachments to the Parliament to carry out such a task. Where a deeper knowledge or more continuous engagement with the task is needed, this would not be feasible.

NEWS GROUPS

One suggestion for information exchange on PAC matters is to make use of news groups. These enable anyone with access to the Internet to contribute information and comment to an international audience. The World Bank runs edited news group systems from time to time on a variety of issues. In January/February 2001 the World Bank and the CPA collaborated on running a news group on oversight and scrutiny issues, possibly a very relevant precursor to a news group on PACs.

A news group can be run as fully administered, with an agency taking responsibility for editing and posting items submitted to it from participants, or it can be run as a free news group that is open to anyone to post material on it directly. The disadvantage with a free news group is that it can attract a large amount of material that is not useful, because either it is repetitive or it is simply irrelevant to the ostensible subject of the news group. On the other hand a fully-administered news group does require an agency willing to accept the editing and administering responsibilities that go with this arrangement. If such an agency would accept such responsibility this may be a cheaper way of disseminating information than using a website.

The Study Group considers that the CPA, in association with other agencies such as the World Bank, should explore the potential for the use of a news group to encourage information exchange on PAC matters.

CONFERENCES AND MEETINGS

The CPA could from time to time run small gatherings, similar in scale to the Study Group meeting, to discuss PAC matters. The CPA's study tours project to promote interchanges between members and staff has already been mentioned. But a more intensive programme on PAC matters is beyond the capacity of the CPA secretariat.

Again the question of branch initiative arises. Commonwealth Speakers, as has been mentioned, have their own regular meetings serviced permanently by the Canadian House of Commons and periodically by the Parliament that is hosting the particular meeting. Delegated legislation committees have regular conferences on a Commonwealth and a regional basis but without necessarily having a permanent secretariat. Regular gatherings of PACs are taking place regionally (Australia, Canada and India are examples), and a Commonwealth PAC association or conference is a possibility to promote interchange of information.

The possibility of a PAC-related meeting at the time of the CPA Annual Conference was considered but is unlikely to be possible. First, there is no guarantee that significant numbers of PAC members will be delegates to the conference and second, the conference already consists of eight sub-conferences (smaller countries, women Parliamentarians and so on) and it would be difficult to fit in another sub-conference. A further suggestion was to hold virtual conferences by staging them through the world wide web. This would have significant advantages in terms of cost savings. The news group ideas already discussed fall into the same category as holding a virtual conference. The Study Group considers that the CPA should examine the possibility of some of the conference options discussed in this section.

COMPENDIUM OF PAC PRACTICE

It was suggested that records of all PACs should be assembled centrally and co-ordinated. This could be done on a Commonwealth-wide PAC database with free access.

However, rather than such information being passively assembled in this way, the Study Group favoured a centrally-managed resource that translated the information received in ways that are useful to PACs. This could take the form of summaries or abridgements of important inquiries undertaken by PACs linked by subject inquired into (education, health, defence and so on) and by activity under scrutiny (purchasing, unauthorised expenditure, public accounts and so on). Such a compendium could also identify legal or procedural issues confronted by PACs in the course of their work. In this way a comprehensive, but accessible, body of information on PAC work and practice could be build up with its results available on the Internet and published or noted regularly in *The Parliamentarian*.

Such work requires a high level of commitment and expertise. It could only be carried out by persons with a knowledge of or familiarity with PAC work and parliamentary processes. It is not, for instance, merely an IT task. The feasibility of such a project depends upon an individual Parliament or branch being willing to accept the responsibility for its development. We recommend that the CPA explore with branches the possibility of one or more of them assembling and producing a compendium of PAC practice.

BENCHMARKING

One particular object of the exchange of information on PACs and Auditors-General is to establish benchmarks for international standards of performance. International auditing associations have set some international audit standards. In this regard Auditors-General have already made considerable progress. The same cannot be said for PACs. Definitions of the essential characteristics and best practices of PACs and Auditors-General in all Commonwealth countries are needed to enable realistic comparisons to be made and to help standards to be improved internationally. Academic research is clearly needed in this area to establish methodologies by which such comparisons can be made, and the Study Group endorses collaboration between universities, Parliaments and international agencies to this end. We hope that this report will itself be an important resource document contributing towards identifying such international standards.

Appendix 1
Commonwealth Parliamentary Association

RESULTS OF QUESTIONNAIRE ON PUBLIC ACCOUNTS COMMITTEES

The figures quoted below are based on the replies of 70 CPA Branches.

1. *What is the size of the current committee?*
   In what proportion do members represent government and opposition?
   In what proportion are government and opposition represented in the House?

Results suggest that the size of a typical PAC in the Commonwealth is eleven members, with the number varying between large and small nations. Asian Parliaments have larger PACs on average (17 members on average), while the average for all Regions of the Commonwealth excluding Asia is nine. Caribbean Region tends towards smaller PACs (six members on average).

Some Parliaments do not have Public Accounts Committees, while others have absorbed the work of a PAC into that of a committee with a much wider remit. This is especially true of small jurisdictions.

In the majority of Parliaments, the proportion of government and opposition Members on Public Accounts Committees reflect proportions in the House: that is, there is a majority of government Members. However, the results suggest that a significant proportion of Parliaments have PACs which are not dominated by government Members. In one Parliament in Africa, for example, all members of the PAC are from the government.

2. *What is the term of office of the Chair and members?*
    Is there any arrangement for continuity by requiring some members to demit office each year?

The term of office of the Chair and members is usually the same as the parliamentary session. However, there are exceptions: in one Canadian Province there is no fixed term for members of the committee, and the term of office in Indian legislatures is typically far shorter than elsewhere in the Commonwealth.

Few Parliaments have formal arrangements for continuity by requiring some members to demit office each year. In one African Parliament, the Speaker reappoints at least one-third of members to the committee each year, and the appointment of members in another African Parliament must include six who were members in the previous year. One Australian legislature reported that four members of the previous PAC had over 26 years' collective experience.

3. *What is the frequency of meetings?*

There are huge variations in the frequency of meetings, ranging from annual meetings in one small Caribbean state to approximately ten meetings every month in a Parliament in Asia. The Caribbean, Atlantic and Americas Region illustrate the differences that can exist in the frequency of meetings of PACs: depending on the location, PACs meet weekly, monthly or even annually. In one Caribbean Parliament there are no set meetings of the PAC.

4. *How is the Chair selected?*
   Is there any constitutional or legal requirement or other convention governing the selection?
   Is the present Chair from the opposition or from the government?

There are many variations in the manner in which the Chair is selected. In India, the normal procedure is for the Speaker to appoint the Chair, while an election is usually held in Canadian Parliaments. Other methods of selection commonly in use include a secret ballot of PAC members and the use of Standing Selection Committees in Africa.

Some Parliaments have constitutional or legal requirements governing this selection (particularly in Canada), but convention and tradition is more common. The Leader of the Opposition is traditionally Chair of the PAC in one Canadian province, whilst the convention in one Australian state is for a government Member to chair the PAC and an opposition Member to be the Deputy. In an Indian State, the Leader of the Opposition or his/her nominee acts as Chair.

Thirty-three per cent of Chairs of PACs in the Commonwealth are from the government while 67 per cent of Chairs are opposition Members. The results suggest that regionally government Members are most likely to chair PACs in Australia (86 per cent) and least likely in Canada and in the Caribbean, Americas and the Atlantic Region. Unlike other legislative committees in one Canadian provincial state, it is customary that an opposition committee member fills the position of Chair, and a government Member serves as Deputy Chair. In another Parliament in Canada, the Standing Orders of the Legislative Council states that "the chairman of the Committee shall be the Leader of the Opposition".

5. *Who determines the agenda for meetings, e.g. Chair, general membership, other arrangement?*

Normal procedure is for the Chair to determine the agenda,

usually in consultation with other sources such as the committee, Secretary of Committee and Auditor-General.

6. *Is it required that the committee be unanimous in its decisions?*

Thirty-three per cent replied 'yes,' and 67 per cent 'no'. Although there is often no requirement for committee reports to be unanimous, PAC reports are usually supported and endorsed by all the committee members. In the Asia Region, 53 per cent of PACs require unanimity when making decisions. No Parliaments from Australia reported that their PAC required unanimity.

7. *Are PAC reports freely available to the general public including civil society?*

Eight-seven per cent responded 'yes' and 13 per cent 'no'. Throughout the Commonwealth, committee reports are usually public documents as soon as they are tabled in Parliament. However, provision is made in some Parliaments for certain reports, or parts of certain reports, to be kept confidential.

8. *Who are normally summoned as witnesses?*

	Yes	No
Ministers	31%	69%
Departmental Officials	97%	3%
Auditor-General	79%	21%
Interest groups/civil society bodies	29%	71%

Note: these are statistics of practice, not of actual cases of those summoned.

There were no examples given of ministers being summoned as witnesses in Asian Parliaments. Other witnesses mentioned were statutory authorities, representatives of government boards and agencies, and academics/specialists.

9. *Are any non-governmental agencies studied by the committee?*

Seventeen per cent responded 'yes', and 83 per cent 'no'.

If 'yes', please give one or two examples,

Those mentioned were development corporations; National Health Service trusts; stock exchanges; telecommunications authorities; industry bodies, academics and statutory boards.

10. *Are hearings open to the press and the general public?*

Fifty-five per cent responded 'yes', and 45 per cent 'no.' Even when hearings are open to the press and the general public, there is usually provision for in camera hearings.

11. *Does the committee depend primarily on the Auditor-General's report?*

Eighty-five per cent responded 'yes', and 15 per cent 'no.'

12. *When is the Auditor-General's report issued: that is, how soon after accounts are presented?*

Replies fell into two categories:

How often the Auditor-General's Report is issued:
More than 10 times a year 5%
3–10 times a year 5%

0–3 times a year	14%
Annually	76%

How soon after accounts are presented:

Simultaneously	9%
Within 15 days of commencement of next session	5%
0–3 Months	3%
4–6 Months	15%
End of financial year	47%
Within 6 months of close of financial year	12%
First quarter of the year	6%
Over 12 months	3%

13. When does PAC commence examinations?

Determined by the committee	16%
After the Auditor-General's Report has been tabled	44%
After projects have been completed	2%
Within a month of the Auditor-General's Report	2%
Between 2–4 months of Auditor-General's Report	12%
Between 5–12 months of Auditor-General's Report	5%
When Parliament is in recess	2%
Other	17%

14. When does PAC report?

Determined by committee (usually at the end of its investigations)	53%
Once a session	12%
Annually	5%
Six months after the Auditor-General's Report	5%
After completion of the Auditor-General's Report	5%
Quarterly	2%
Other	18%

APPENDIX 1

15. *Is the PAC report debated in the legislature?*
    If so, how is it debated?

Fifty-seven per cent responded 'yes', and 43 per cent 'no.' In the Indian legislatures, PAC reports are not normally debated in Parliament. PAC reports are generally debated through a motion being tabled or through a committee of the whole House. In practice, however, the extent of the debate usually is limited (for example, committee members will just speak to the report), and many reports are adopted without debate.

16. *Is the executive required to respond to PAC recommendations?*

Eight per cent responded 'yes', and 20 per cent 'no'. Results suggest that the executive is less likely to be required to respond to PAC recommendations in Canada regions. In an Australian Parliament, the responsible minister must respond to the recommendation of a committee within three months, or alternatively give an interim response at three months and a final response within six months. The minister must table the response in the Parliament.

17. *What are the staffing/facilities available to the committee?*

A Clerk/Secretary with various levels of additional administrative, research and technical support is usually available to the Committee. As might be expected, the facilities available to Parliaments in small countries are less comprehensive, but significant variations were difficult to discern. However, facilities in two African Parliaments were described as 'very basic', and computer facilities appear less common in African Parliaments. Some PACs have exclusive staffing and offices; however it is also common for PACS to share their resources with other committees in Parliament.

18. Is there any mechanism in place for the measurement of performance?

Thirty-three per cent responded 'yes', and 67 per cent 'no'. Common mechanisms in place for measuring the performance of PACs are Annual Reports and corporate/business plans with performance indicators and targets. Results suggest that PACs are far more likely to have their performance measured in Africa (47 per cent) and Canada (50 per cent).

19. Has there been any recent study or comment on strengths and weaknesses of the operations of the committee?

Eight per cent responded 'yes', and 92 per cent 'no'. The working of the PAC was considered at a Conference of Chairmen of Central and State Public Accounts Committees at Parliament House, New Delhi on 17 and 18 January 2001. Other comments generally derive from the media: it was reported in the media of one Caribbean country, for example, that the PAC was not as effective as it should be.

APPENDIX 1

NOTE

Number of replies:	70
Africa:	18
Asia	17
Australia	8
British Islands and Mediterranean	6
Canada	10
Caribbean, Atlantic and Americas	6
Pacific	1
South-East Asia	2
Anonymous	2

Appendix 2
Battling corruption: strengthening Parliament's oversight role

Forty-seventh Commonwealth Parliamentary Conference, plenary session summary, Canberra, Australia, September 2001

Parliamentary and legal mechanisms to prevent, expose and punish public corruption, including improper conduct by Parliamentarians themselves, must be put in place and then firmly enforced and regularly updated, both to conserve resources for development and to raise public confidence in the political process, argued Mrs Cheryl Gillan, MP, of the United Kingdom in opening the first section of the initial plenary session during the 47th Commonwealth Parliamentary Conference held in the Parliament of Australia in September 2001.

Labelling public corruption as a key issue, Mrs Gillan challenged Commonwealth Parliaments to make the abuse of the citizens' trust a high-ranking crime. Parliaments should fully use their watchdog role and their positions as legislators and representatives as a focus for strong anti-corruption programmes as part of the popular global demand for good governance. The conference, which began its formal sessions in the Great Hall of the Australian Parliament in Canberra, was attended by approximately 520 delegates, secretaries and observers from 156 Branches of the Commonwealth Parliamentary Association.

The British Member lamented that there was currently no end in sight to instances of abuse of power and of corruption in both developing and developed governments, even though these illicit activities often led to loss of life by denying resources to governments and inflating prices for key goods, such as medical supplies. She acknowledged that there would always be some in any organization who would abuse their positions; but every organization had a responsibility to minimize the opportunities for abuse and to expose and punish it when it occurred. Transparency International kept an index of corruption for public officials and politicians, she said, noting that her country ranked 13th on the list.

As the representatives of the people, Parliamentarians had a particular duty to maintain the highest levels of integrity, she said. Being seen as rogues who bought or influenced their way to power would only undermine their position as public watchdogs.

MAKING THE RULES WORK

While calling for the creation of anti-corruption mechanisms where they did not exist, Mrs Gillan noted that most Commonwealth countries and Parliaments already had anti-corruption procedures in place. It was, however, necessary to use them effectively and to update the mechanisms and systems constantly to cover new ways to abuse power and circumvent the rules. It was especially important to ensure that anti-corruption bodies themselves were kept free of dishonesty.

She said public service must respect its core values: impartiality, legality, transparency, integrity, full accountability and the provision of just, honest and efficient service. These values should be fully reflected in throughout the governmental system, including in parliamentary rules on the declaration of Members' interests. It must be constantly made clear that public office must not be used for private gain.

Mrs Gillan said direct corruption and some indirect forms of corruption were already commonly covered by criminal law. These provisions should be firmly enforced. Sound ethics management systems and scrutiny and reporting mechanisms should be fully in place, effective and accessible, including whistle-blower protection. Most countries had various procedures, but she argued that they were seldom sufficiently well developed.

The Member added that anti-corruption and good governance programmes should take advantage of technological developments and should include education programmes as part of a movement away from enforcement toward prevention.

LOOKING AHEAD

Mrs Gillan expressed the hope that the conference's workshop on this subject would help Members to answer a number of critical issues which would face Parliaments and Parliamentarians as they grappled with measures to raise standards in public life.

Who should conduct anti-corruption investigations and were procedures to warn, fire and prosecute corrupt public officials sufficient? How should Parliamentarians and ministers be dealt with most effectively, and did giving amnesties for former regimes work, she asked.

Did Parliaments have effective procedures to scrutinize the executive through debates, questions, committee investigations and direct challenges? Were women less prone to corruption than men?

Were sufficient controls in place to stop smuggling, embezzling, siphoning off funds, buying personal goods with public money, manipulating share prices and other forms of corruption, she asked.

Mrs Gillan concluded that those in government must set high standards of conduct in order to enable administrations to deliver good governance to the people.

COMMONWEALTH DIVERSITY

Dr Frank McField, MA, of the Cayman Islands, cautioned that a Parliament was a reflection of its community's social, economic and cultural values. Those who preached anti-corruption measures must respect the moral standards of other communities and understand how a Parliament interacts with its society.

He raised the issue of what he described as the assault by the Organization for Economic Co-operation and Development and other large interests on small states, some of whose economies were dependent on the offshore finance industry. Politicians needed to carefully consider what all Commonwealth countries were doing to ensure democracy and development for all and to prevent multinational companies and groups of countries from subjugating small states.

A Mauritian Member, Dr the Hon. James Burty David, MP, agreed, asking when the world would criminalise what he said was the international highway robbery of small states. Corruption should be redefined to include the activities of multinationals and large intergovernmental agencies which drained the wealth from small and developing countries.

From India, Smt. Ambika Soni, MP, said consideration had to be given to the different social and economic backgrounds of MPs. She suggested that the power to recall MPs would encourage them to behave better.

Smt. Soni also called for changes to election financing arrangements. Maintaining that MPs commonly overspent and used resources they should not to get elected, she said consideration should be given to state funding of election campaigns so candidates did not mortgage themselves to win office.

Appendix 3
Strengthening Parliament's role in the battle against corruption

Forty-seventh Commonwealth Parliamentary Conference, workshop report, Canberra, Australia, September 2001

The session was opened by Mrs Cheryl Gillan, MP (UK) who introduced the theme of the session. The facilitators who provided papers to stimulate session discussions were Mr A. J. Leon, MP (South Africa), Mrs Patricia Gordon-Pamplin, JP, MP (Bermuda), and Dr Talalelei Tuitama Leao, MP (Samoa).

Mr Leon's paper noted that politicians the world over tended to be regarded as corrupt, a perception which could best be countered by improvements to the framework of accountability. Mr Leon outlined ways of improving accountability by providing the answers to a series of questions. Firstly he noted that there must be a political culture of Ministerial responsibility and accountability, and that this must be also shared by the heads of government. For example, there should be sufficient opportunity for Ministers and leaders of government to be made publicly accountable during parliamentary question time. A second key question was whether there was a Public Accounts Committee and whether there was a developed, bipartisan committee system in existence.

Jurisdictions should ask themselves whether they followed international best practice in this regard. He pointed out that there should be a registrar of Members' interests and an Ethics Committee with wide-ranging investigative powers.

Mr Leon noted that another important question to be answered was whether majority parties abused their positions or whether Legislatures were in the position to stand up to executive power. Opposition parties needed to be accorded respect if a system was to be open and accountable.

Other important safeguards against political corruption within jurisdictions were an adequate anti-corruption legislative framework which criminalised the misuse of public office, the protection of 'whistle-blowers' within the bureaucracy, and freedom of access to government information. Also crucial was a free press.

It was also important to set out standards or codes of conduct whereby legislators could regulate their conduct with respect to conflict of interest situations.

Finally Mr Leon noted that all countries faced the problem of corruption, it was recognised as a world wide problem and that it was not culturally relative.

Mrs Patricia Gordon-Pamplin, MP (Bermuda) addressed the problem of corruption by noting firstly that it was important for all politicians to eliminate corrupt behaviour on a personal and individual level. Respect for politicians and for political institutions is ultimately dependent on the collective ethical behaviour of individual politicians.

Mrs Gordon-Pamplin said that not only politicians but public servants must be made accountable for their actions and must adopt an anti-corruption culture if respect for the institutions of government was to be maintained. It was up to Parliament to enforce rules governing the behaviour of politicians and officials and to stamp out cronyism. One useful method of assuring accountability was the declaration of Members' interests. A publicly available register enables the assets of Parliamentarians to be verified. Its accuracy is important and there should be legislated penalties for non-compliance and wilfully inaccurate statements.

Mrs Gordon-Pamplin also noted the importance for parliamentary accountability of parliamentary committees, particularly of Public Accounts Committees (PACs). It was important that PACs have wide powers to examine papers and persons. In some jurisdictions the Auditor-General sits as an ex-officio member of the PAC. Other important anti-corruption safeguards were adequate remuneration for public servants and the open disclosure of political campaign funding.

Finally it was vital to realise that individual vigilance on the part of politicians was necessary if a culture of corruption was not to overwhelm respect for democratic institutions. Mrs Gordon-Pamplin noted that corruption could undermine the development priorities of countries.

Dr Talalelei Tuitama Leao, MP (Samoa)), the third facilitator, spoke of corruption as a disease and noted that its causes must be identified as a priority. Causes of corruption which varied in emphasis amongst jurisdictions included the lack of moral vigilance among politicians to curb materialistic impulses, also lack of accountability, religious and cultural factors, the complacency of over-secure governing parties with the corresponding weakness of oppositions, and the lack of judicial independence.

Dr Leao cited among possible parliamentary cures for corruption bipartisan investigatory committees that had the power to scrutinise annual reports of government departments, and the power to call for persons and papers. It was also important to educate both MPs and electors in their democratic rights and responsibilities. The live broadcasting of parliamentary sessions was an important aid in this respect. It was important to cultivate a respect for the idea of public service within a jurisdiction to counter the culture of corruption.

Mrs Gillan opened the floor for discussion, and the meeting heard comments from more than 34 contributors. The first speaker was Dr Frank McField (Cayman Islands), who pointed out that different countries have different ethical perspectives on corruption. For example it could be argued that competition engendered corruption. Corruption was shaped by cultural and social environments. Shri P. M. Sayeed (India) reinforced the view that corruption was the enemy of good governance and that Parliaments were the custodians of probity in public life. Parliaments were in the position to combat corruption by setting up frameworks of anti-corruption legislation, as had India. Important elements were freedom of information legislation and anti-corruption investigatory agencies. MPs could reduce corruption through ethics committees, committees of members' interests and committees of privileges. Consistent vigilance against corruption was important.

Sen. Paul Calvert (Australia) noted the importance of an independent and powerful upper house as an important safeguard against governmental corruption. He also noted the importance of a comprehensive committee system including estimates committees. He made reference to other accountability factors such as a strong opposition and the use of question time to make ministers publicly accountable. He noted the Australian use of registers of Members' interests, the Charter of Budget Honesty Act, the independent offices of Electoral Commissioner and Auditor-General and the judiciary. He cited Australia's political disclosure laws, whistle-blower legislation and public servants' code of conduct as important aids to accountability.

The Hon. Ngamau Munokoa (Cook Islands) noted the importance of educating citizens in the principles of good government if democracy was to flourish. Politicians needed reminding to be responsive to the needs of their electors.

Mr Greene-Lulilo Mwamondwe (Malawi) said that poverty made corruption inevitable and that the practice of presidential appointments was a factor that encouraged corruption in some jurisdictions.

The Rt Hon. Mamora (Lagos) agreed that poor people saw public office as a chance to enrich themselves and that culture resulted in bad governance. Electors in such jurisdictions saw their elected representatives as satisfying their personal needs and not those of the electorate as a whole.

Mr Nigel Evans (UK) drew attention to the cynical attitude of electorates towards politicians in many countries. He noted that corruption caused disenchantment with politicians across the board. For this reason it was important for democratic institutions to be on their constant guard against corruption. A vigilant free press was important for this. Transparency of the public appointments process and a select committee system independent of executive government through non-government committee chairs, were other important elements. Transparency of electoral funding and of the electoral process were also crucial factors in guarding against corruption.

Smt. Margaret Alva (India) also agreed with previous speakers that corruption was part of the human condition and said that politicians should not accuse each other of corruption for political gain. Corruption had its origins in poverty and existed on a global basis. The press also suffered from corruption. Mr Bernard Navakobi (Papua New Guinea) agreed about the inevitability of corruption and said that the key to fighting it was the adequate funding of organisations to expose and punish corruption within jurisdictions. Mr Arthur Anae (New Zealand) said the greatest responsibility in the fight against corruption lay with politicians themselves, who had a duty to set a good example in their personal behaviour. Shri H. K. Patil (India) noted that the beneficiaries of corruption were the rich and its victims the poor. The CPA should wage a war against corruption. Legislation could ensure transparency and accountability of governments and reduce the discretion of bureaucrats to engage in corrupt practices. Democracy must ensure the education and empowerment of the masses of citizens so that they can control those in authority over them.

Mr Georgiou Aristophanes (Cyprus) said that the same ethical standards should apply to all levels of society and government without exception. Major John Kazoori (Uganda), Sen. the Hon. M. L. Peete (Lesotho) and Mr S. K. Kar (Orrisa) all noted the importance of an international effort against corruption which must be seen as a global problem. International seminars for MPs such as the present forum were a useful start. The Hon. E. D. Mnangagwa (Zimbabwe) cited bureaucratic structures, the overcentralization of decision making and poverty as the most serious sources of corruption, and agreed with previous speakers that national and international strategies to combat corruption must be adopted by jurisdictions. Shri Singh Sadanand, MLA (Bihar), the Hon. Inder Singh Namdhari (India) and the Hon. N. S. Pharande, MLC (India) noted the existence in India of the Central Vigilance Commission legislation of 1999 as an important anticorruption tool and emphasized the fact that legislators have the prime responsibility to set a good example. Also political parties should set about fighting corruption within their organisations. Brig. Hon. B. Pezzutti (New South Wales) also drew attention to the existence in NSW of the Independent Commission Against Corruption, the Police Integrity Commission, Royal Commissions and parliamentary Codes of Conduct as important anti-corruption mechanisms. Mr Firoz Cachalia (Gauteng) focused on the role of Parliament and said that Parliaments were structurally unable to deal with corruption themselves because of the close relationship between government parties and the executive. Also the adversarial nature of the parliamentary system cut across its ability to hold executives accountable. Other independent accountability structures were required. Shri Sathir Singh Kadian (India) and Dr the Hon. Amir Gama Zainab (Tanzania) agreed that leadership was important in combating corruption and that incorrupt leaders were essential in a parliamentary democracy.

Sen. Gillian Lucky (Trinidad & Tobago) noted that legislation to support integrity in public life should be enacted and enforced. It was important to recognise that corruption was a global phenomenon and that the media were an important watchdog against corruption. There should be ethical training for political parties. Shri Sardar C. Atwal (Punjab) agreed. The Hon. Sipho W Lubisi (South Africa) and the Hon. K. Malua (Tuvalu) noted the importance of a culture of political integrity. Political parties had a responsibility to select people of integrity to be elected representatives. The importance of a comprehensive committee system for parliamentary accountability was also noted. Mr Chew Heng Ching (Singapore) gave the view that the fact that Singapore had only had one party in power since independence showed that its system was free of corruption. He noted that good government was a product of the meritocratic selection of candidates for office and the payment of public servants at private sector market rates. Payment of politicians in Singapore depended directly on the efficient functioning of the economy.

The Hon. Mustafa Bin Ali (Malaysia) drew attention the importance of religion in setting suitable ethical standards to combat corruption in all jurisdictions. the Hon. Joseph Mbah-Ndam (Cameroon) agreed that it was important to combat corruption on a global basis. The Hon. Joseph Hiram (Nauru), however, pointed out that in some jurisdictions electors still expected their representatives to supply personal favours.

In summing up the session Mr Tony Leon (South Africa), Mrs Patricia Gordon-Pamplin (Bermuda) and Dr Talalelei Leao (Samoa) noted that everyone was agreed as to the evil of corruption and the importance of combating it. In the developing world it was important to recognize that corruption deters investment. The individual ethics of leaders and Parliamentarians were also important in fostering anti-corruption cultures in all jurisdictions.